GAEL CHANDLER FILM EDITING

GREAT CUTS EVERY FILMMAKER AND MOVIE LOVER MUST KNOW

Published by Michael Wiese Productions
3940 Laurel Canyon Blvd., # 1111
Studio City, CA 91604
tel. 818.379.8799
fax 818.986.3408
mw@mwp.com
www.mwp.com

Cover Art by MWP
Book Layout: Gina Mansfield Design
Editor: Paul Norlen

Printed by McNaughton & Gunn, Inc., Saline, Michigan
Manufactured in the United States of America
Printed on Recycled Stock

Library of Congress Cataloging-in-Publication Data

Chandler, Gael, 1951-
Film editing : great cuts every filmmaker and movie lover must know / Gael Chandler.
p. cm.
Includes bibliographical references and index.
ISBN 978-1-932907-62-9
1. Motion pictures--Editing. I. Title.
TR899.C46 2009
778.5'35--dc22

2009013319

To Maggie Ostroff (1935-2008),
film lover and assistant editor who began her career at the age of 47,
true friend, in and of the cutting room

&

To all moviegoers who desire to understand editing
or begin editing at any age.

CONTENTS

FOREWORD

As part of the research for a film I made called *The Cutting Edge: The Magic of Movie Editing*, I read many books on the subject. No matter how inspiring or helpful, it was often problematic visualizing the magic and the mechanics of edit points described by text alone. And that's understandable given how difficult it is to detect the cuts even when we are watching a movie.

Cinema editing has traditionally been called the "invisible art." That invisibility in a well-edited film helps to keep us seamlessly engaged in the story and world of the movie. But aspiring filmmakers and curious moviegoers have a natural inclination to want to know how films are put together.

One of the most refreshing contributions of *Film Editing: Great Cuts Every Filmmaker and Movie Lover Must Know* is to make these imperceptible edit moments visible. Emmy-nominated editor and author Gael Chandler accomplishes this by artfully arranging great still frames from popular feature films to illustrate editing tactics used by Hollywood pros.

Designed in the tradition of the comic strip, this book is a lively compendium, or better yet, a "pictionary" that catalogues types of cuts editors employ in storytelling. Chandler's straightforward text distills the classic use of powerful editing conventions. For example: Charming shots from the movie *Cars* and compelling frames from *Babel* of Pitt and Blanchett support text that outlines how eyeline matches influence match cutting. Stills from *Crash* and *Pan's Labyrinth* show match action cutting, another aspect of continuity cutting that Chandler includes. Sequences from *The Diving Bell and the Butterfly* and *The Constant Gardener* illustrate different ways jump cuts have been used. The scope of techniques covered is broad and inclusive from match cutting to time shifts and from effects cutting to parallel action and beyond.

Although there are no rules in the formidable and complex art of movie editing, cutting practices like these have evolved over the last 100 years of trial, error and discovery in editing rooms throughout the world. They have become part of the basic grammar of film and are tools filmmakers, be they official students or self-taught home moviemakers, should understand and experiment within their own work.

Ultimately great editing is about the artistic intuition that shapes the story, understands the psychology of a character relative to the performance of an actor, and is sensitive to nuances of key emotional moments that provide the magic we see on the screen. A grounding in the building blocks (craft) of editorial construction that this visual toolkit provides will give filmmakers the tools they need to realize their creative ideas and will serve as a springboard for invention.

Chandler's insights into how edits are used to excite audiences to laughter and tears or make bad cuts work will also delight every moviegoer who enjoys being a sophisticated entertainment consumer.

From an instructional design standpoint, this book offers film teachers a clear-cut and economical approach to traditionally complex material. This book is a valuable resource with great ideas for movie clips that demonstrate and contextualize editorial concepts.

By taking a visual approach to a visual medium, Gael Chandler's accessible digest makes an exciting contribution to the literature on editing. It's clear that she loves the movies, knows her craft, and has a methodical mind that provides us hard-won clarity on the elusive art of editing.

Wendy Apple

Award-winning producer/director of *The Cutting Edge: The Magic of Movie Editing* (BBC, NHK, STARZ! and Warner Brothers' Home Video); *Hard Rain* (NBC), starring Bob Dylan; *Appearing Nightly* (HBO), starring Lily Tomlin; TVTV's *Lord of the Universe* (WNET/Alfred I. Dupont-Columbia Journalism Award); *Five Easy Steps to Metaphysical Fitness* (a comedy), executive produced by Bob Balaban and Emily Levine and featuring award-wining scientists like Danny Hillis and Kary Mullis. Adjunct professor of Cinematic Arts at USC.

PREFACE

Editing is like flying; it's hard to say how it's done even when you're doing it or watching it on the screen. We fly in our dreams or see others fly in the movies and perhaps can state the mechanics of flight, but we struggle or become poetic when attempting to describe the feeling and effect of actually flying.

This book aspires to show the types of cuts that editors make and at the same time to describe what effervesces from those cuts — the marvelous, mysterious magic that continues to beguile audiences. If you are a moviegoer and always wanted to be able to spot a subliminal cut in a movie, detect a bad cut or greenscreen effect, or appreciate how an action scene's fast pacing is created, you will learn to recognize these cuts, effects, and scenes and many more. If you're a filmmaker — professional, student, or doing your own thing for YouTube, family, or friends — this book should inspire you to use and experiment with cuts you haven't previously tried and help you better understand those you have made.

For me, writing the book has deepened my knowledge, appreciation, and enjoyment of movies and of how editing makes its own magical reality from the filmed creations of the writer, director, cinematographer, and actor. To everyone who reads this book, I wish you the same experience: enjoy your flight!

ACKNOWLEDGMENTS

Writing a book is like making a movie: impossible to do by yourself. I am supremely thankful to:

Mimosa Andre, Brennan Jackson, Katie McCord, and Sarah McCord for pointing the way to what gen YouTube is watching.
Jay Scherberth, Glenn Farr, and Jan Ambler for astute editorial input.
All the editors, directors, and filmmakers whose work fills the frames of this book.

David Couper and George Rowbottom for insightful reading.
Larry Gross for lending DVDs of movies I would never have otherwise seen or included.
Marcy Rothenberg, Ilene Haber, and Mike Cuffe for the time.

Gina Mansfield for being a joyful partner and expertly laying out the book.
Ken Lee for imperturbably handling the myriad of large and small logistics as always.
Michael Wiese for the inspired assignment and belief that went along with it.

Sherry Green for everything — from the subliminal and daily to the mindful and ever-lasting.

PERMISSIONS

The author acknowledges the copyright owners of the following motion pictures from which single frames have been used in this book for purposes of commentary, criticism, and scholarship under the Fair Use Doctrine.

INTRODUCTION

Editing gives film its meaning and its effect.
— Filmmaker V. I. Pudovkin in his book,
Film Technique and Film Acting

Whether performed in a drab, musty, studio editing room, a disco-lit editing bay, a cubicle, a closet, or a classy pad above the Pacific — and I've cut in them all — editing invariably takes place in a space shaded and lit so the filmed images can be most clearly seen.

The editor's job is to take the raw material — camera footage — and put it together to make the best piece possible, be it a comedy, drama, music video, documentary, or commercial. The editor accomplishes this by making cuts — placing one shot after another. Cut by cut, the movie builds, until, if well-edited, it becomes more than the sum of its cuts.

Why does an editor make a cut? Simply stated; to drive the story forward and show the audience what it needs to know at each moment. With every cut, the editor determines what the audience learns next about the story, characters, or subject. No matter what the genre — drama, thriller, documentary, horror, biopic, action-adventure, samurai, anime, or comedy — the editor's mission is the same. Every cut is a building block of the movie and bridges to the next cut. The editor, like an architect, designs each cut to support the entire film. With every cut, the audience learns, senses, thinks, or feels something different.

This book shows the different types of cuts and how they affect the audience so that you can recognize them when you watch a movie or video — including one you've edited yourself — and judge their effectiveness. It describes each type of cut and illustrates it with frames from all genres of recent movies (except for Hitchcock's *Rope* from 1948). The film frames — in pairs and groups — are arranged to read from left to right and from top to bottom. For a synopsis of each film portrayed in the book, turn to the page after the last chapter. Terms and concepts are defined as they arise, but if there's a term you're not clear on that isn't defined, check the Glossary, located after the Synopsis of Films.

Here's a quick preview: We'll start with basic cuts, then look at cuts that use effects such as dissolves, wipes, and greenscreen. Along the way we'll discuss mismatches, jump cuts, and why cuts don't work as well as smash cuts and subliminal cuts. We'll then delve into editing for rhythm and pacing and finish by focusing on what's behind the conventions — flashback, montage, parallel action, etc. — of edited scenes. So… lights down, roll film: Let's see what's created in the usually ever-so-humble editing room.

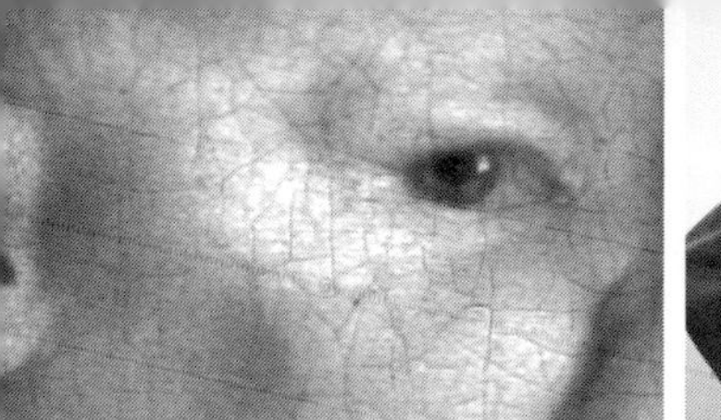

chapter 1 BASIC CUTS

The art of editing occurs when the combination of two or more shots takes meaning to the next level – excitement, insight, shock, or the epiphany of discovery.

– Professor Ken Dancyger from his book *The Technique of Film and Video Editing*

In this chapter we'll cover common cuts that are seen in every movie. These cuts form the basic language of film editing; you will spot them in the rest of the book's chapters. So what exactly is a cut? Read on.

CUT

The joining together of two different shots; or occasionally, two parts of the same shot.

Every cut must be motivated; in other words, the editor must have a reason for making it. A cut builds story, idea, or emotion, changes the point of view, or keeps the pace going: In fact a cut may do some or all of these things.

BASIC CUT: Two shots edited together.

In Shot 1 islanders cross a bridge.

In Shot 2 a sentry with a spear watches the bridge.

Pirates of the Caribbean: Dead Man's Chest

REVERSE CUT

A cut to the opposite (reverse) angle. The cut can be from the front *of a character to the angle* behind *the character (Reverse 1) or vice versa. Or the cut can be* from *a character (or characters)* to *the character (or characters) they're facing (Reverses 2-4).*

REVERSE 1:
This reverse cuts from behind the boy as he aims for the tourist bus on the highway below to the front of the boy.

Babel

By showing how characters act, react, and interact, reverse cuts keep the audience involved in the action and dialogue. Reverse cuts also often demonstrate the dialectic dance of opposition as characters confront, confound, and cuddle each other.

REVERSE 2:
Walking the mall.

Crash

REVERSE 3:
In the chapel, The Bride introduces her ex-lover (left) to her groom (right).

Kill Bill: Vol. 2

REVERSE 4:
Watching a play.

Finding Neverland

POV (POINT OF VIEW)

A reverse cut that corresponds to where a character is looking; a POV is a cut to what the character is seeing.

POV 1:
Miners lower a bucket into a well, hoping for oil. The second frame is the POV shot.

There Will Be Blood

A POV is a highly motivated cut; a character sees something and the audience wants to see it too. *The Diving Bell and the Butterfly* contains approximately 20% POV shots as Jean-Do, its main character, is immobilized by a stroke.

POV 2
(selected cuts):
Jean-Do emerges from a coma and sees medics. The first frame is the POV shot.

The Diving Bell and the Butterfly

Look! He's waking up.

Do you remember what happened?

POV 3:
Spying the pirates down the beach.

Pirates of the Caribbean: Dead Man's Chest

Matching the angle on a POV is critical to the audience's accepting the connection between the character and what they are seeing.

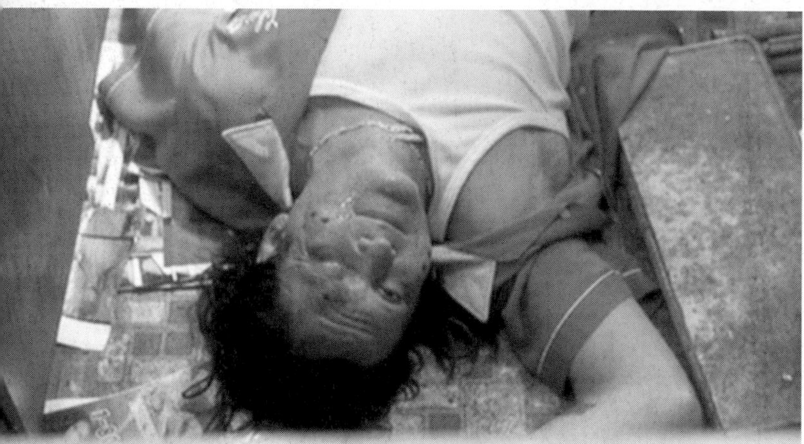

POV 4:
Dying man and his eye-patched killer.

Kill Bill: Vol. 2

A mirror is a perfect device for slipping in a POV.

POV 5:
In his truck's side view mirror, one cowboy eyes another.

Brokeback Mountain

POVs are often framed by an object such as a window, gun sight, a pair of binoculars, or windshield (POV 6-7) ...

POV 6:
Scanning
for rebels.

Pan's Labyrinth

POV 7:
Driving into chaos.

War of the Worlds

…even a monocular or a colander will do (POV 8-9).

POV 8:
One-eyed Moody puts the eye on Harry and Ron.

Harry Potter and the Goblet of Fire

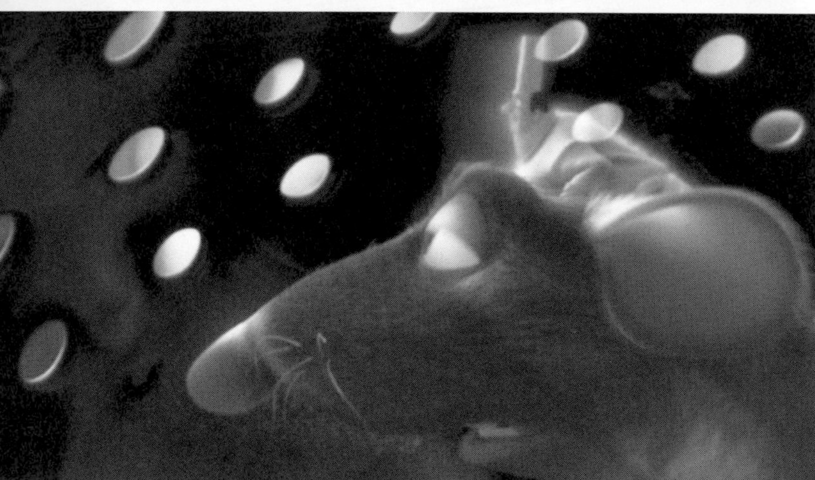

POV 9:
Little Chef (the rat) watches the action from inside a colander.

Ratatouille

REACTION

A cut to a participant reacting to something that has just happened.

REACTION 1 (selected cuts): Reacting to rivals plunging into the drink.

Pirates of the Caribbean: Dead Man's Chest

Editing in a reaction or series of reactions can be extremely powerful as reactions show human emotion and thought, and key viewers' emotional response: Should they hold their breath, laugh, cry, worry, or get angry?

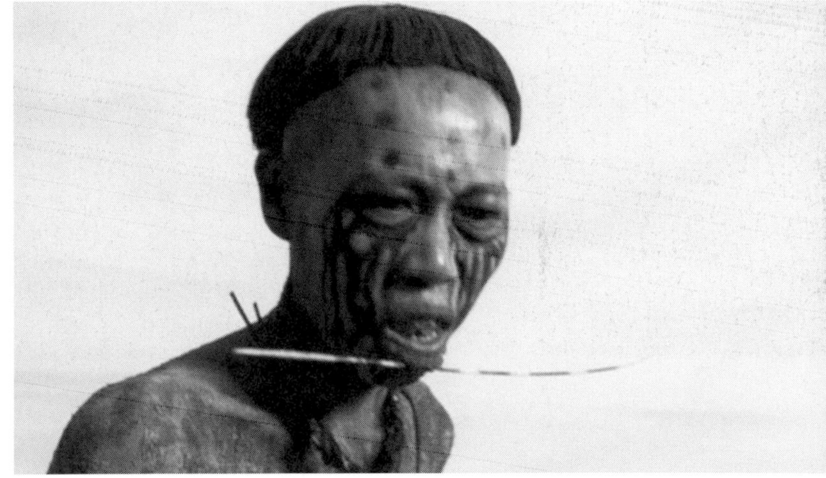

Frequently, it's more important for the audience to see people reacting rather than see what's happening.

REACTION 2 (selected reactions): The World Trade Center falls.

Director Michael Moore chose to show New Yorkers reacting instead of the towers collapsing.

Fahrenheit 911

REACTION 3:
In the middle frame, the leader of the Israeli anti-terrorist squad listens to his team during their lighthearted "get acquainted" lunch. As the movie's main character and conscience, he observes and reacts in this and many other scenes in the movie.

Munich

The same goes for dialogue (conversation) scenes: Watching the listener react can be more significant than watching the speaker.

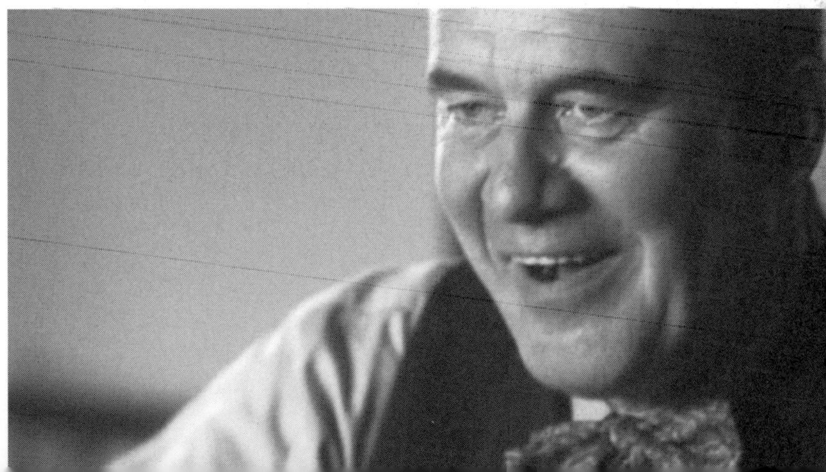

Cutting in a series of reactions can also intensify the drama.

REACTION 4:
A child is reprimanded; his parents and prospective in-laws react.

Corpse Bride

REACTION 5: Who's the bride's daddy? The three candidates react along with the mother in this climactic wedding scene.

Mamma Mia

Lastly, cutting to a reaction can eliminate dialogue or narration.

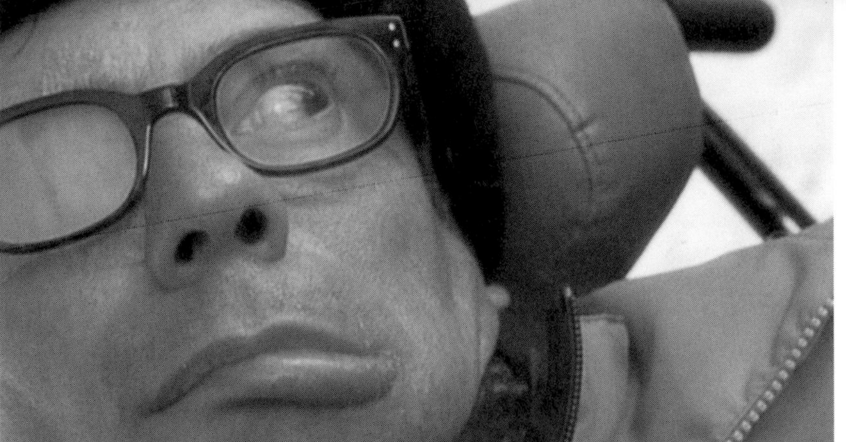

REACTION 6: Jean-Do (left) fears what his children will think seeing him for the first time after his stroke. We see the answer in their reactions – faces and thoughts – expressed in the English subtitles.

The Diving Bell and the Butterfly

INSERT AND CUTAWAY

These terms are used interchangeably to describe a cut to a small, significant detail of a scene. A classic example is a cut to a letter or some form of writing, as exemplified in Cutaway 1. Note: These terms are also used freely as nouns and verbs.

CUTAWAY 1: This cutaway to a postcard (middle frame) forms the crucial response that re-unites the society-crossed lovers.

Brokeback Mountain

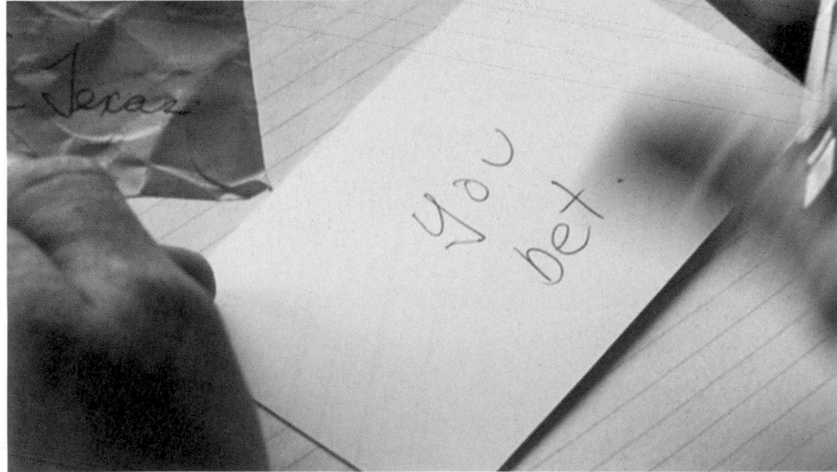

Primarily, inserts/cutaways serve to convey necessary information to the audience (Cutaways 2 and 3).

CUTAWAY 2: Checking the tracking device.

No Country for Old Men

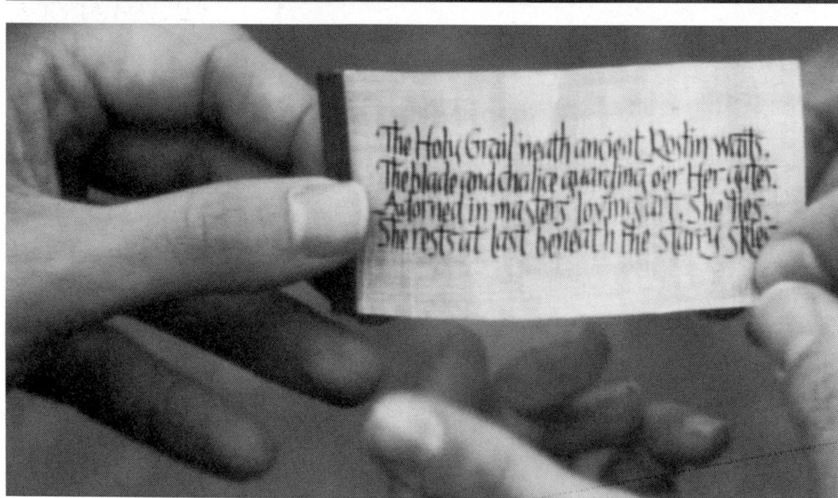

CUTAWAY 3: Reading a clue.

The Da Vinci Code

CUTAWAY 4:
The insert of the title on the door shot (middle frame), efficiently moves the story from the exterior establishing shot (top frame) to right inside the meeting (bottom frame).

The Bourne Ultimatum

Commonly, they act as introductions to scenes (Cutaway 4) or segues between scenes (Cutaway 5), forwarding the flow of information — usually scene location or time — and the action.

LONDON THEATRE REVIEWS

LITTLE MARY by J.M. Barrie

MR BARRIE'S PLAY FAILS TO IMPRESS

Cast List

CUTAWAY 5: A clever, literal cutaway! A shot of J. M. Barrie and wife at his play's opening night is followed by a cutaway to his maid cutting out the poor review.

Finding Neverland

CUTAWAY 6: Cutting away to the mother and child bridges dialogue between the pair of two-shots of the couple on the couch.

Fahrenheit 911

Editors routinely cut away to shorten time or bridge between two mismatched shots. In dialogue scenes, especially in documentaries, reaction shots are often inserted to skip over unwanted dialogue and advance the action.

Lastly, cutaways can cleverly comment on the action as this scene from *The Da Vinci Code* illustrates.

CUTAWAY 7: Pursued by a killer, a museum curator makes a desperate run for his life, passing paintings which reflect his distress and doom.

The Da Vinci Code

SOUND CUT

In addition to story and performance, there are two things editors always consider when cutting:

Picture – framing, lighting, movement, angle
Sound – dialogue, narration, sound effects, and music

Sound contributes to a movie in numerous ways — emotion, rhythm, tone, realism — to name but a few, and is integral to the audience's acceptance and enjoyment of the film. Since our focus is on cuts and because sound is difficult to see, especially on the page, we'll concentrate on how sound influences the cut.

Sound is one of the main motivators of cuts. For instance, an editor may cut to the words a person is speaking before cutting to the speaker. Why? Usually to show the listening character reacting to the words and to keep the story zipping along. If every piece of a dialogue starts and finishes on the person delivering it, the pace of the show lags and the audience simply tunes out.

Walter Murch, picture and sound editor of numerous movies and Academy Award winner for *Apocalypse Now* and *The English Patient*, asserts, "Whatever virtues sound brings to the film are largely perceived and appreciated by the audience in visual terms — the better the sound, the better the image."

In this opening scene from *The Bourne Ultimatum*, winner of the Academy Award for editing in 2007, we see how an offscreen sound — sound we don't see the source of on screen — makes a character react and motivates a cut.

SOUND CUT 1a: The thriller begins with edgy music as a tense Bourne heads to the Moscow train station.

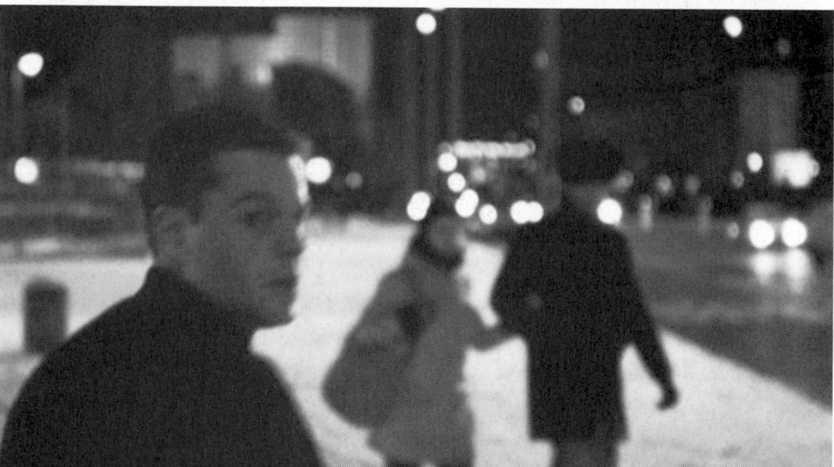

SOUND CUT 1b: Part way into this cut an offscreen sound motivates his head turn. Who's there?

SOUND CUT 1c: We glimpse the source of the sound — a police car approaching from the distance.

The Bourne Ultimatum

Sound plays a pervasive and critical role in *Slumdog Millionaire*, slam dunk 2008 Academy Award winner for editing, directing, best picture, and more. As the movie's hero relives the sights and emotions of his brutal childhood and interrogation by the police, the sounds make the events all too real and cause the audience to recoil.

SOUND CUT 2 (Selected shots): The sound of lightening takes the sleeping boy back to a riot and the malice of a Molotov cocktail thrower. We hear the smash of the bottle, the whoosh of the flames, and the screams of the boy's mother as she burns up before his eyes and exhorts him to flee.

Slumdog Millionaire

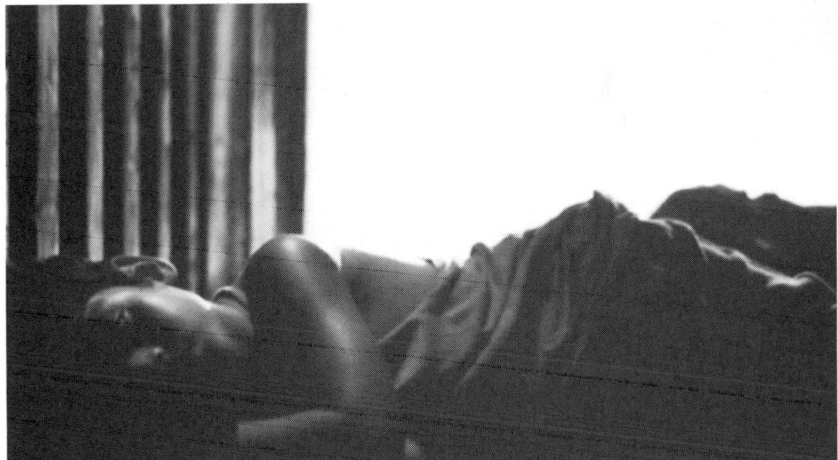

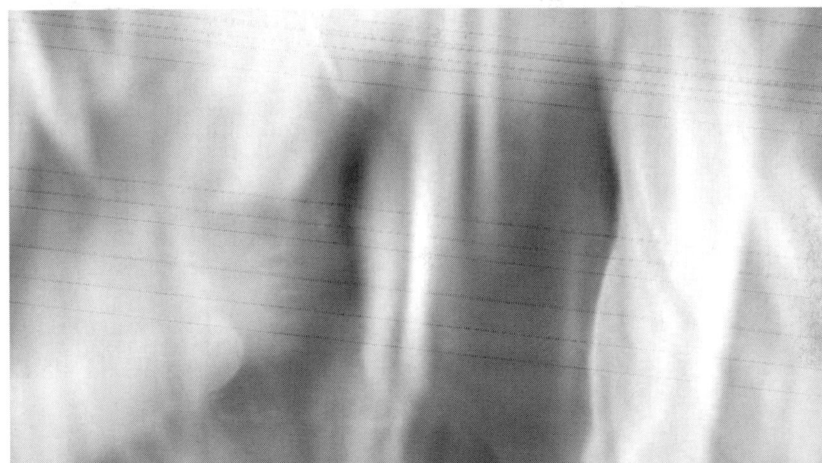

WRAP UP

Now that you're familiar with basic cuts and cutting language, we'll move on to the next chapter and cutpoints — places in shots where editors choose to make cuts. We'll talk about how the audience reads these cuts and what makes cuts successful.

Note: If you're editing your own project, before reading on, you may want to review your work to see if you've used — or might want to use — any of the cuts described in this chapter. You can consider reviewing your work after each chapter.

chapter 2 MATCH CUTS

How do editors decide where — at which frame — to cut from one shot to another? They usually look for a match point, meaning a place in the first shot that is duplicated in some way in the second shot. There are many elements that need to match and usually are matched: screen direction, eyeline, camera angle and framing, props, sound, weather, wardrobe, hair, make-up, lighting, color, and action.

Match cuts comprise the majority of cuts editors make. Why? Because match cuts push the story forward seamlessly, maintaining the continuity — physical relationships (characters, props, background, etc.) and narrative flow — of the action. Match cutting makes for such smooth cuts that the audience doesn't notice them. This "invisible" editing, as it's called, leaves the audience engrossed in the story and its characters — precisely the editor's intention!

When cuts don't match and continuity is broken, the audience may become lost and lose interest in the movie, if only momentarily. Filmmakers want their work to be seen and bring a profit. They don't want the editing (or anything else) to make the audience stray from the movie, decide they don't like it, and tell others.

Now that I've stressed the importance and frequency of match cuts, be assured that match cutting is not an editing rule. The rule is to serve the story and the subject. Many cuts that work do not match. In the next chapter we'll discuss mismatches and look at examples from a few superbly edited movies.

In this chapter we'll go over the most critical elements that editors match cut.

SCREEN DIRECTION MATCH

Matching screen direction means matching how a character (or object) exits one shot and enters the next shot, reappearing where the audience expects to see them. Huh? Here's an example: If a character moves right out of a shot, they need to enter the next shot from the left of the frame so they look like they're continuing to move from left to right as depicted in the example below.

1

2

SCREEN DIRECTION MATCH 1:
Car takes off (frame 1), exits in a cloud of dust on the right (frame 2) and reappears on the left (frame 3).

Cars

Note: Frequently, the character will not appear for a few frames in either the outgoing shot — first side — or incoming shot — second side — of the cut. To best illustrate how screen direction is matched, our examples will show characters and objects in frame on each side of the cut.

3

SCREEN DIRECTION MATCH 2:
Paprika, the young heroine of this anime movie, slyly demonstrates screen direction by chasing a human robot toward a movie screen.

Paprika

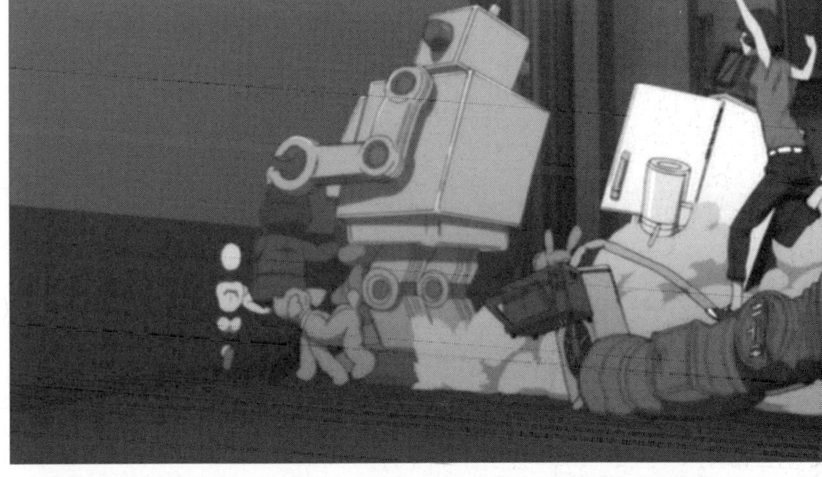

SCREEN DIRECTION MATCH 3:
In city clothes, J. M. Barrie exits left followed by a friend (frame 1). He enters right as a pirate (frame 2), changing time, place and costume in one match cut.

Finding Neverland

EYELINE MATCH

Matching the lines of vision between characters' eyes.

If eyelines don't match, viewers take a different meaning from a cut, so it had better be what the editor intended. Usually non-matching eyelines mean the characters are avoiding or disregarding each other for one reason or another.

EYELINE MATCH 1: Two counter-terrorists converse. It isn't always necessary to match eyelines on phone calls, but it helps.

Munich

EYELINE MATCH 2: Even cars' eyelines match.

Cars

These three cuts are from a scene in *Babel* between a married couple. The nonmatching eyelines in Cuts 1 and 2 demonstrate how they have become disconnected after the death of their baby. The matching eyelines in Cut 3 show them beginning to grapple with their pain and each other.

ANGLE MATCH

Matching shots with similar angles such as long shots, medium shots, close-ups, etc.

When two characters (or objects) are interacting, especially in dialogue scenes, the editor will often match angles, especially as the scene reaches its climax. This keeps the story taut and the characters closely connected.

Pictured below are two dialogue scenes with typical angle matches. Notice how the eyelines are maintained here too.

ANGLE MATCH 1: A pair of matching over-the-shoulder shots.

No Country for Old Men

ANGLE MATCH 2: Matching the father's POV of his daughter.

Crash

ANGLE MATCH 3:
Skewed angles at the beginning of this movie warn that something's off kilter.

The Constant Gardener

ANGLE MATCH 4:
A pair of tilted angles accentuates danger and chaos as a minion of villain Lord Voldemort menaces Harry.

Harry Potter and the Goblet of Fire

FRAMING MATCH

Matching the space around the characters — how they are positioned and framed.

Normally, framing matches involve matching angles of shots: wide shots, medium shots, close-ups, etc.

FRAMING MATCH 1: These wide, over-the-shoulder shots form a match cut that incorporates the scene's atmosphere and location while keeping the focus on the sheriff and his deputy.

No Country for Old Men

FRAMING MATCH 2: In this pair of raking shots, Howard Hughes pitches his first film to a dismissive studio executive.

The Aviator

FRAMING MATCH 3: Notice the large amount of off-center, matched space on this cut between J. M. Barrie and his wife at a dinner party.

Finding Neverland

SHAPE MATCH

Matching similarly shaped objects or forms.

SHAPE MATCH 1: Victor Van Dort (left) eyeballs his future in the eye socket of a skull.

Corpse Bride

While not necessary for continuity, a shape match is a fun cut to spot in a flick or to make yourself when editing. Shape matches can also predict or comment on the action and are often used to span time and/or place.

SHAPE MATCH 2: A cloud produced by headlights in town at night matches a cloud created naturally on the veldt during the day.

The Constant Gardener

SHAPE MATCH 3: Circular shapes are the most common type of shape match.

Pan's Labyrintha

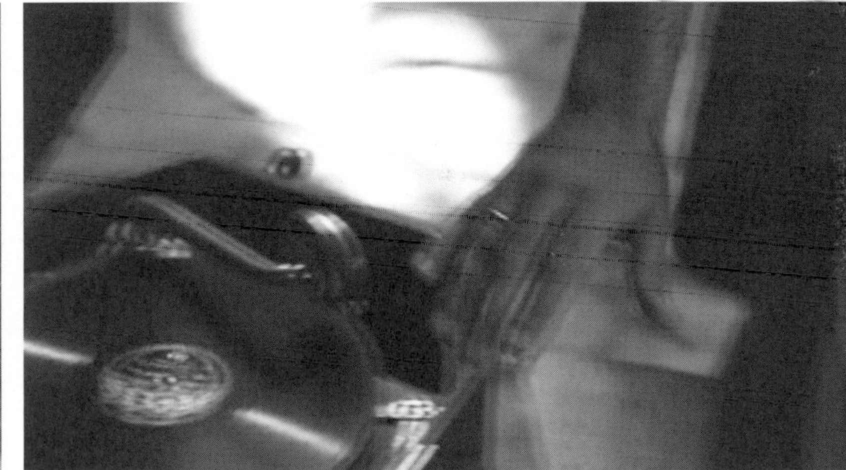

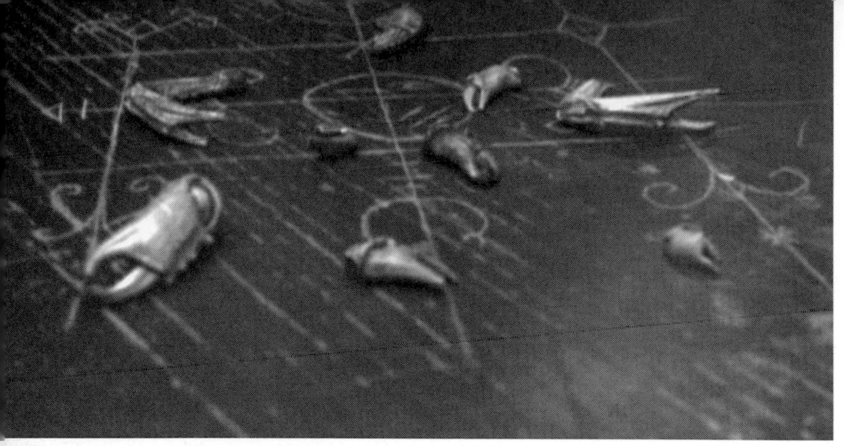

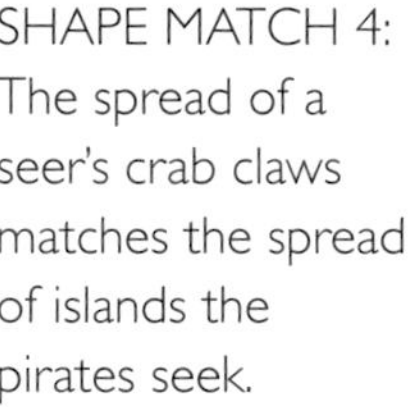

SHAPE MATCH 4: The spread of a seer's crab claws matches the spread of islands the pirates seek.

Pirates of the Caribbean: Dead Man's Chest

SHAPE MATCH 5: A train snakes through country-side, then cars wind through city streets as Bourne closes in on his contact.

The Bourne Ultimatum

LIGHTING AND COLOR MATCH

Matching color and lighting between cuts.

Seems simple, but due to having to film at different times in varying weather, lighting and color regularly don't match upon arrival in the cutting room. This is why every show budgets for color correction. This involves making sure the color and lighting match from cut to cut and within each scene. Color correction takes place in a computer or film lab once the show is locked (the editing is finished and approved). If color and lighting are not matched, the audience may conclude that time has passed or a location has changed. The result: Misinterpretation of key information and the interruption of the seamlessly edited story.

LIGHTING MATCH 1: Matching day lighting on the set.

Spider-Man 2

LIGHTING MATCH 2: Matching night lighting at the campfire.

Brokeback Mountain

COLOR MATCH 1:
The main character backpacks through the golden hue of sunset on the plains.

Into the Wild

COLOR MATCH 2:
Vampires battle werewolves in a subterranean world of blue in this movie.

Underworld Evolution

COLOR MATCH 3:
Red dominates this scene where Howard Hughes shuts out a friend (right) during a mental breakdown.

The Aviator

ACTION MATCH (A.K.A. MOTION OR MOVEMENT MATCH)

Matching the action (movement or motion) of characters or objects in one shot to the action in the next shot where the action continues or completes.

ACTION MATCH 1: Normally, an action match on a door opening takes a character from inside to outside (or vice versa) or from one room to another. This exceptional door opening match cuts between two scenes and two characters: It shows one character leaving a store during the day and another character exiting a different store at night.

Crash

The action may be as mundane as a character turning their head or entering a door or as fantastic as a starship hurtling through space, it doesn't matter: Action matches are among the most common yet dynamic of all cuts.

Why do action matches work so well? Because viewers' eyes follow motion, no matter how slight or grandiose, and miss the cut, once again making for seamless editing. The action match also moves the story forward, literally. Equally importantly, action match cuts maintain a scene's pacing, be it fast, medium, or slow. (More on pacing in Chapter 6: Cutting for Rhythm, Pacing, and Time.)

ACTION MATCH 2: The sight and sound of cascading water advances the flow of the story.

Pan's Labyrinth

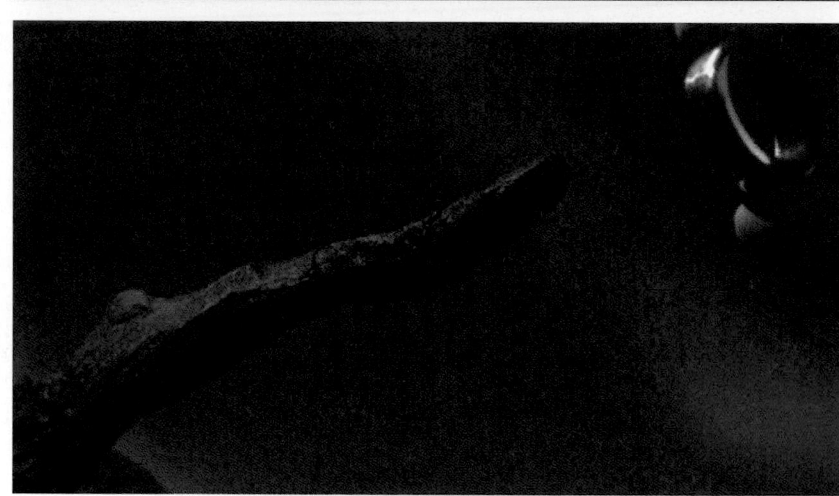

ACTION MATCH 3: This action match creates the pivotal moment of the movie when Victor slips the ring onto the corpse bride's finger, mistaking it for a twig.

Corpse Bride

Action match cuts can take the story from one scene, place, time, or world to another.

ACTION MATCH 4: A cut on action joins these two scenes where one man exits down a hotel staircase with a suitcase (left) and another man enters a kitchen with a brisket (right).

Munich

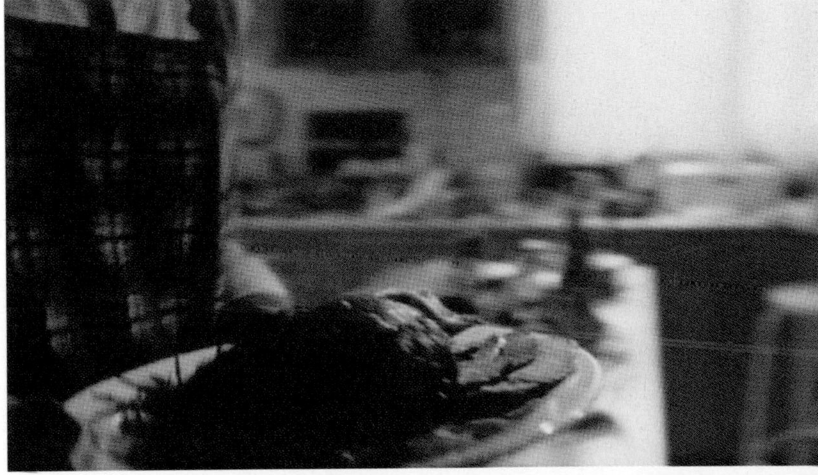

ACTION MATCH 5: J. M. Barrie dances into a fantasy world in this whirling action match between scenes.

Finding Neverland

ACTION MATCH 6:
A pair of matching zoom-in shots perfectly fits the story as the girl enters the labyrinth.

Pan's Labyrinth

Action matches also occur when an editor cuts from one moving camera shot to another moving camera shot. The camera movement — pan, track, zoom, etc. — repeats in the next shot.

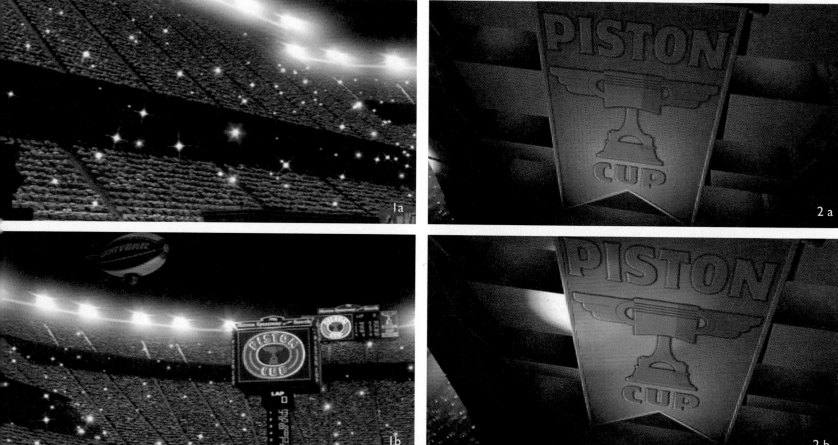

ACTION MATCH 7:
A car race — shown in a series of panning, zooming, and tilting shots and accompanied by a pop song — kick starts this movie. To illustrate the movement of the camera, the first and last frames of two shots are pictured.

Shot 1 pans right, across the stadium and stops on the blimp. Shot 2 tilts up, bringing the sign and the crowd on the ground closer.

Cars

IDEA MATCH (A.K.A. CONCEPT CUT OR RELATIONAL MATCH)

Two shots edited together that create an idea, insight emotion, or character trait. The sum of the edit is more than the two shots in themselves.

IDEA MATCH 1: Howard Hughes explores his lover's back in the same meticulous manner he uses to inspect the body of his latest plane prototype.

The Aviator

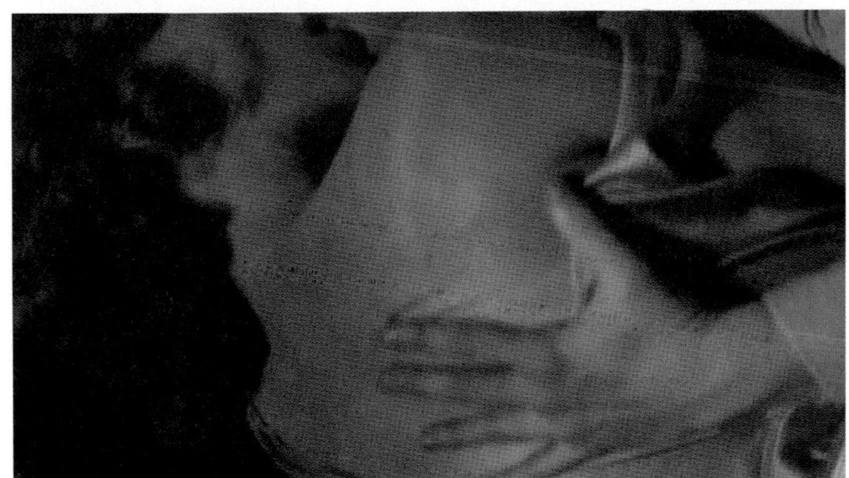

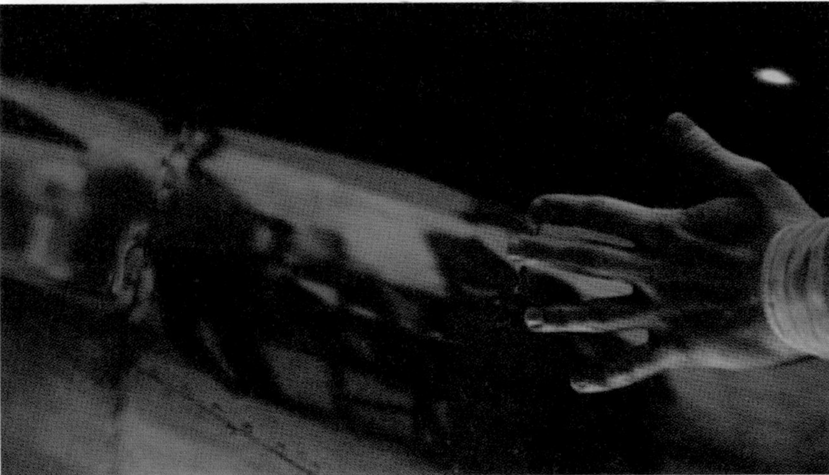

An idea match can span place, time, character, or subject to forge a connection or motivate a change. Familiar examples would be a clock running down to signify a character's death or a band of soldiers rallying after glimpsing their country's flag.

An idea match can also make a subtle comment, foreshadow events, or plant ideas.

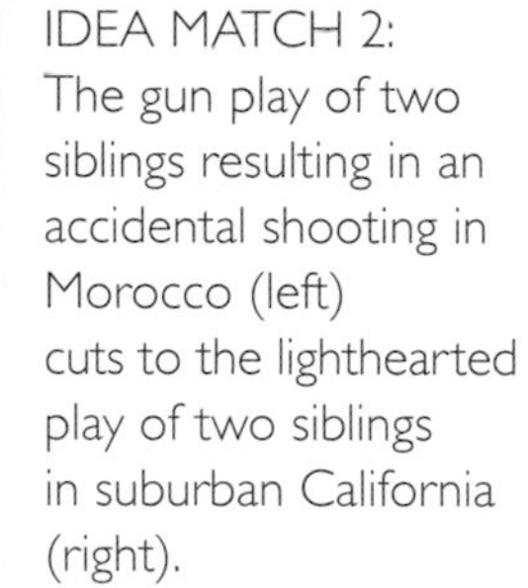

IDEA MATCH 2:
The gun play of two siblings resulting in an accidental shooting in Morocco (left) cuts to the lighthearted play of two siblings in suburban California (right).

Babel

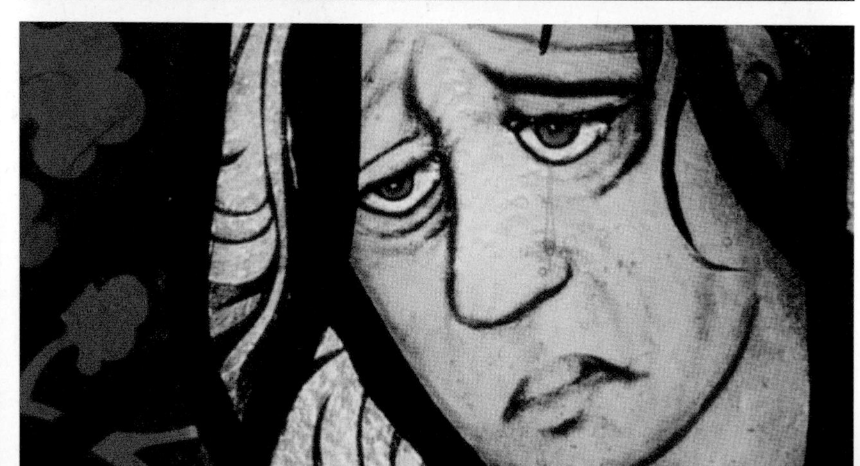

IDEA MATCH 3:
Neville, Hermione, and Harry head downstairs during a rainstorm as the figure in the stained glass appears to weep, foreshadowing a fellow student's death, in the movie's climactic scene.

Harry Potter and the Goblet of Fire

SOUND MATCH

Matching two similar sounds. The sounds can be voices, sound effects, natural sounds, rhythm or musical passages.

SOUND MATCH: The sound of the welder soldering (top left) cuts to the sound of the dentist drilling (below).

Man on Wire

Like shape matches, sound matches customarily cross time and/or place and are a delight — or sometimes a fright — to encounter. The two related sounds can insinuate a different meaning or spin the story in a different direction. Often the first sound — an innocent, everyday sound — is intensified, changed, or distorted by the second sound. For example: The pop-pop-pop of children playing war cuts to the real thing; the quiet chinking of car chains in the snow becomes the harsh staccato of bottles moving through a processing plant; or the patter of rain gradually morphs to the patter of applause. In *Apocalypse Now* Francis Ford Coppola cut from the whirr of ceiling fan blades to the roar of helicopter blades.

Matching sound across a cut can connect the two shots in an unexpected way and make the audience laugh, wince, or seize up with fear. Viewers appreciate sound matches and may never think of certain sounds the same way again.

ROPE MATCH

Matching two different takes of the same camera angle.

This elusive match cut pays homage to director Alfred Hitchcock, whose 1948 movie, *Rope*, depended on them. To understand the concept and how Hitchcock employed it, a couple of definitions are in order:

> *Master shot, a.k.a. master* — Shot that encompasses all the action in a scene, from beginning to end. Although a master often starts framed close on a small object and can move as needed to capture the action, it mostly stays wide to frame all the action.
>
> *Coverage* — All angles filmed in addition to the master: close-ups, medium shots, POV shots, etc. Coverage provides editing choices and allows the editor to cut freely between masters.

Hitchcock took on the job of directing *Rope* as a "stunt" in his words. The stunt was to mimic the original British stage play by filming the movie version on one set in real time. Limited by the ten-minute length of a 35mm camera roll, the 81-minute film is actually composed of ten reels, ten masters, ten cuts, one establishing shot of Manhattan, and no coverage.

The cutting was premeditated by Hitchcock and executed in the camera. In an interview with director Francois Truffaut in 1966, Hitchcock recalled, "The mobility of the camera and the movement of the players closely followed my usual cutting practice. In other words, I maintained the rule of varying the size of the image in relation to its emotional importance within a given episode."

Rope matches are impossible to detect if done properly; I know, as I've made them. Since the cuts in *Rope* are well documented and easy to detect once you get the hang of them, we'll take our example from *Rope*. Hitchcock's editor invariably added a few black frames to soften the match between masters, but a rope cut can work without black frames if the camera work is consistent. To demonstrate this, I've deleted the black frames.

Rope most often uses a character's back to end one master shot and cut to another, as seen here.

ROPE MATCH CUT: SHOT 1. (frames 1-3) Shot 1 has the character cross the room (frames 1-2) and pause with his back to the audience (frame 3) to end the shot and initiate the cut.

ROPE MATCH CUT: SHOT 2. (frames 4-6) Shot 2 starts where Shot 1 ended: with the character's back to the audience (frame 4). Shot 2 then continues as the character exits frame and reveals another conversation (frames 5-6).

Rope

WRAP UP

Match cuts, continuity, and invisible editing: Now that they make sense, let's look at some cuts that are anything but invisible! These rebel cuts break continuity and can jump out at you — they're rogues! But do they work? Turn to the next chapter to see, and, if you're a filmmaker, to determine how you might use them when editing your own film.

The Japanese will never know there's another
heaven above the Emperor's head.

chapter 3 ROGUE CUTS:

MISMATCHES, JUMP CUTS, CROSSING THE LINE, AND BAD CUTS

Editors regularly cut shots together that were filmed in different locations at different times by different crews. Mismatches happen. Not because the editor isn't paying attention to which hand holds the knife from one cut to another but because the editor is paying attention to where the story is going and where the audience's focal point will be. Yes, the editor is a magician of sorts, finessing mismatches and other non-continuity cuts to keep the audience's attention and the story clocking along. As director/editor Edward Dmytryk wrote in his book *On Film Editing*, "Film is the art of illusion, and the most unlikely things can be made to seem real."

In this chapter we'll expose mismatches from a few well-edited movies — half of which won or were nominated for the Academy Award for editing — and discover how the editors mitigated the mismatches. We'll also explain jump cuts and their many functions in movies. Lastly we'll define crossing the line and the 180° rule — a mystery to many filmmakers — and discuss what a bad cut really is.

MISMATCH

A cut in which continuity is lost due to a difference between elements such as action, eyeline, lighting, camera framing or position, props, weather, wardrobe, or makeup.

A mismatched cut can cause confusion, but more often than not, viewers miss the mismatch due to the skill of the editor. Mistakes in continuity — and getting around them — are part of daily life for editors. How do they do it? By keeping continuity of other elements — usually action or sound (sound effects, music, and/or dialogue) — and concentrating on propelling the story forward.

The following mismatched cuts from popular movies show how editors sustain continuity of other elements to shift the viewer's attention away from the mismatch.

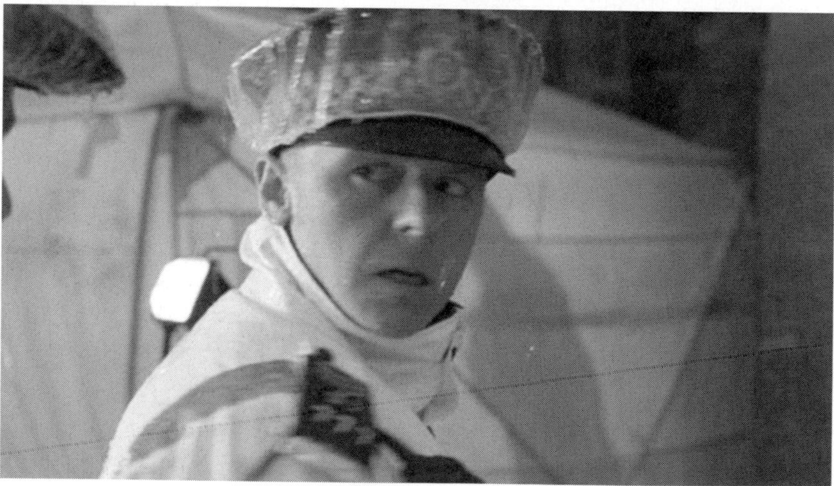

MISMATCH 1: Someone got left out of the rain. The second shot contains none but since his rain cap shows raindrops, the cut is short, and it's the last shot in a gray scene, it splashes by.

Hot Fuzz

The next few examples deal with actors and mismatches and how editors work around them. Ralph Winters, editor of *Gaslight*, *The Pink Panther*, *10*, and *Victor Victoria* and other movies, believes, "Nobody [no actor] does anything twice the same way, so the trick is to get [cut] in and out at those times when you don't think an audience is going to be disturbed… You put them where you want them to be. They'll watch action, they'll watch movement."

MISMATCH 2: The background continuity and motion of the falling leaves obscures the sword mismatch — pointing down in first shot, up in second shot — of the striking warrior.

Hero

MISMATCH 3: The mismatch of the actor's hand (absent in first shot, grasping phone on second shot) is masked by the change in camera angle and the continuity of the girl's piano playing.

Munich

MISMATCH 4:
A literal sleight of hand by the editor. Both the left-hand position of hatless Howard Hughes and the background action are mismatched in this cut. However, the brisk camera movement and dialogue disguise the mismatches in this Academy Award winner for best editing.

The Aviator

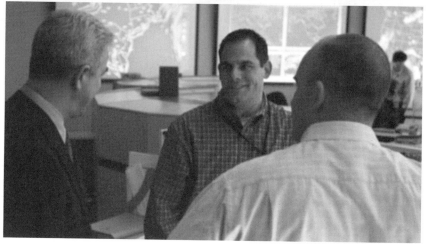

MISMATCH 5:
The head positions and eyelines of the actors in the first shot don't match those in the second shot. Again, the dialogue, pacing, and actors' performances smooth these mismatches.

United 93

MISMATCH 6:
Getting goats or a crowd of people to match is impossible. But the movement of the herd, along with the lighting and screen direction matches, carries the viewer's eye and obliterates the mismatch.

Babel

MISMATCH 7:
Can you count the mismatches in this confusing cut? See below for answer.

Cars

There are four mismatches: Screen direction, position (sports car), background, and foreground. The movement of the sports car to the front of the line helps keep the focus off the confusion.

JUMP CUT

A cut where objects or characters appear to jump because the shots are so similar. Technically, this is due to the camera angles of the two shots being less than 30° apart.

JUMP CUT 1: Using jump cuts in lovemaking scenes has reached cliché status, which is mocked in this film as Jean-Do lets his imagination carry him away.

The Diving Bell and the Butterfly

Jump cuts are disorienting by nature; they counter continuity and shaft seamless editing. This is why they were spurned by Hollywood and traditional U.S. filmmakers for decades. In the 1950s and 1960s, French New Wave directors famously embraced jump cuts and they were then taken up by independent U.S. filmmakers. Nowadays jump cuts are accepted, used, and appreciated for what they bring to movies: Few action scenes, horror movies, video games, and music videos exist without them.

William Chang, who edited *Red Dust*, *Ashes of Time*, *In the Mood for Love*, and other films, states that, "A movie, by its nature, has to economize the usage of time to tell a story. I view a jump cut like any other cut — its function is to economize."

Jump cuts are employed in a myriad of ways: To make dramatic points, shorten time, express a character's thoughts, perceptions, dreams, or nightmares, and to add or subtract a person or object from a shot, to name but a few.

JUMP CUT 2:
In this scene of multiple jump cuts, a widower remembers a time of joy when his expectant wife set up their baby's room prior to its stillbirth and her murder. Even though this cut jumps him from foreground (frame 1) to the background (frame 2), the near match of her hands, the lighting, and the strong connection of the actors make this jump cut work.

The Constant Gardener

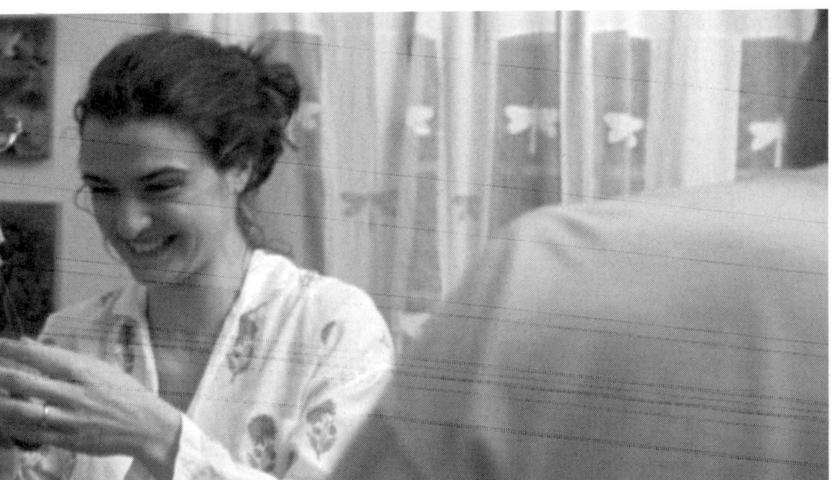

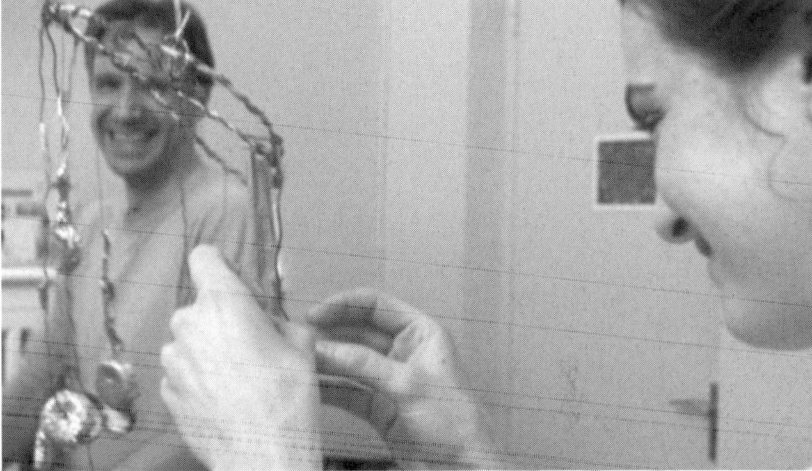

JUMP CUT 3:
A clown car leaps into frame via a jump cut at the beginning of this innovative anime film.

Paprika

JUMP CUT 4:
Jump cuts shorten time as the pirates advance across the wide expanse of sand and sea.

Pirates of the Caribbean: Dead Man's Chest

JUMP CUT 5:
The silhouetted lecturer pushes a slide projector's remote button and click! He jumps forward and to the left side of the screen.

Hot Fuzz

JUMP CUT 6:
Three pairs of jump cuts increase the intimacy and sense of passing time as Jean-Do shaves his 92-year-old father.

The Diving Bell and the Butterfly (selected cuts)

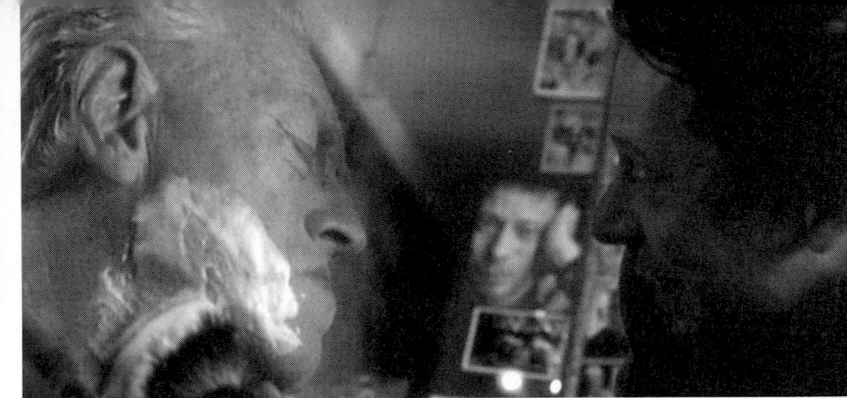

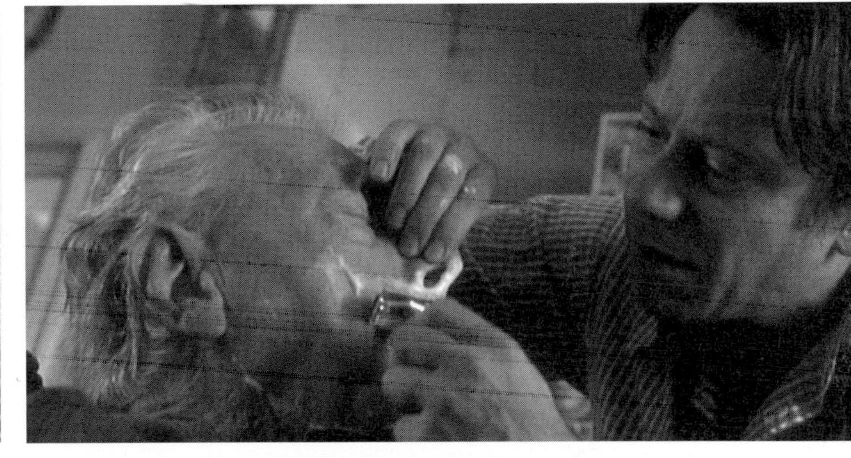

CROSSING THE LINE THE 180° RULE

There is an invisible line in every camera set up that bisects the scene horizontally at 180 degrees. If the camera crosses this line, it breaks the 180° rule, and viewers can lose their reference to where people and objects are in the scene.

Disorientation works fine for war and other chaotic scenes but in most situations, crossing the line can confuse and lose the audience. For instance, if the camera shoots from both sides of a football game, sports fans will be mixed up about which team is going in which direction for the goal. For this reason, sporting events are routinely filmed from one side of the game.

If all this seems a bit murky, let's turn to *Paprika*, named for its redheaded heroine, a young girl who is also unclear on the concept. The subtitles and shots provide the answers.

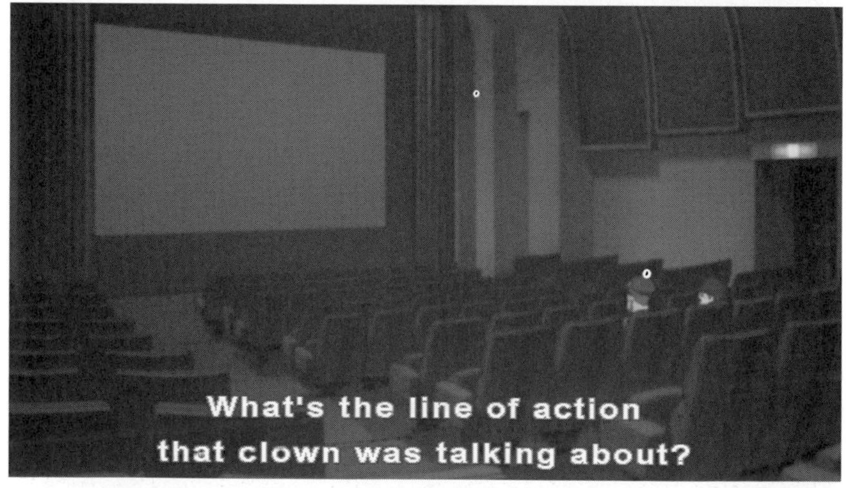

Cut 4 crosses the line and breaks the 180° rule. Why? Because the girl (Paprika) appears to be on her director friend's right side when she's clearly on his left side in cuts 1-2. Cut 5 correctly observes the rule: Paprika appears to be on his left. Notice that the characters do not change positions or eyelines: Keeping their geography clear relies on filming according to the 180° rule.

Paprika

It's an imaginary line...
1

...that connects the subjects on camera.
2

If the camera crosses that line...
3

...the cut is awkward.
4

That's why it has to be like this.
5

Directors film footage from both sides of the 180° line. So how do editors take the audience from one side to the other of the line? There are three main ways to manage this, as the next few pages illustrate.

Managing the 180° Line with a Cutaway 1: In the first shot, a play with two actresses is watched by a family, visible in the background. The middle shot — a cutaway to a spectator — creates a smooth cut to the third shot where the actresses are seen from the audience's POV. Eliminating the middle shot would cross the line, potentially baffling the film audience with the swap of the actresses' positions.

Finding Neverland

Managing the 180° Line with a Cutaway 2: In this tense scene with a lot of players, the cutaway to an overhead shot bridges to the third shot, avoiding crossing the line and keeping the audience from losing all sense of the scene's geography and its players' positions.

Munich

A second way to observe the 180° rule is for the director to tell the actors to move.

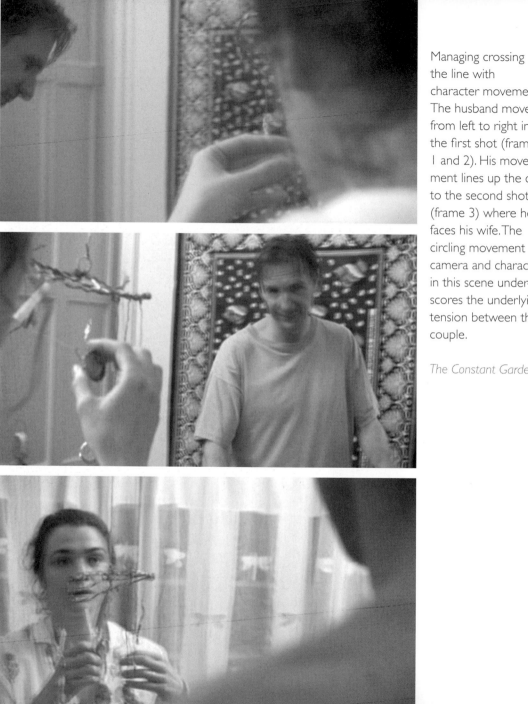

Managing crossing the line with character movement: The husband moves from left to right in the first shot (frames 1 and 2). His movement lines up the cut to the second shot (frame 3) where he faces his wife. The circling movement of camera and characters in this scene underscores the underlying tension between the couple.

The Constant Gardener

The Japanese will never know there's another
heaven above the Emperor's head.

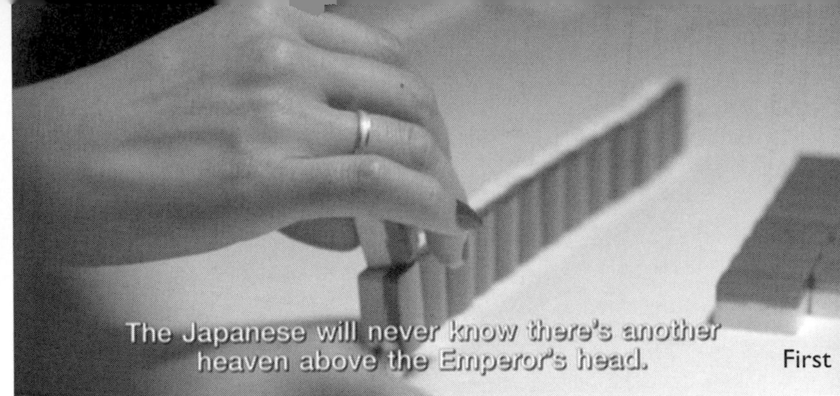
The Japanese will never know there's another
heaven above the Emperor's head.

First

The third way to avoid crossing the line is for the camera to move. The camera breaks the 180° line and creates a new one once it stops moving. This method keeps the audience riveted to the action and allows the editor to cut in other shots, as this scene from *Lust, Caution* demonstrates. The first and last cuts are cutaways; the three middle cuts show the camera circling clockwise around the mahjong table.

Come on, eat. While it's hot.

I really shouldn't...I'm so fat already.

I really shouldn't...I'm so fat already.

Last

In this last example of crossing the line, the editor simply ignores that the line has been crossed. Disorientation is not a problem since the audience is totally immersed in the movie and the music is playing in this MTV style cut. After all, who cares? The hero has just won 20 million rupees in an arduous TV contest, triumphed over a life of poverty, crossed several railroad tracks, and relived forced separation from his true love. Here, in these final two shots of the movie, the lovers are united with their first kiss. The cut brings them from a shadowy yellow light into a bright white light as they break the 180° rule and break away from their past to embrace the dawn of their life together.

Managing crossing the line with camera movement: The climactic moment and last cut of this movie cross the line and no one notices. Why? Because the editor shows the audience what it needs and wants to see: The full faces of the couple as they are finally able to express their love for each other.

Slumdog Millionaire

BAD CUT

A cut that does not move the story forward and risks disengaging the audience from the movie.

It could be a perfectly matched cut of two gorgeous camera shots and still be a bad cut. Why? If the cut doesn't move the story forward — by giving new information, changing the locale, or building the drama, idea, or emotion — it doesn't serve the audience or the movie and is a bad cut.

For these reasons it is impossible to show a bad cut; it must be recognized within the context of a movie. So how do you detect a bad cut? If you find yourself bored, confused, or suddenly aware of the movie theatre or your life and not the movie, a bad series of cuts, perhaps adding up to an unnecessary scene, has probably led you there.

Why are there bad cuts? There are a few reasons. The editor may be a novice who puts in too many shots that go on too long or fly by too fast and generally do not show the rhyme or reason for the story — its heart and soul. Secondly, bad cutting occurs when the editor's voice and skill are thwarted by the higher authority of an inexperienced director, producer, or client. Ordinarily, editors do not have final say on the cut, so cuts and scenes can be kept in that bog down the movie and beg to be eliminated or more tautly edited. Lastly, the script may be full of holes or the footage may be so insufficient or inferior that there isn't enough to construct a proper scene.

WRAP UP

Next time you're watching a flick or viewing your current project, challenge yourself to look for good cuts and bad. This will enhance your moviegoing experience and help in evaluating your own editing work. Now we'll make a jump cut of our own to the arena of effects. We'll start by defining the ordinary effects you'll see in most movies.

chapter 4 CUTS THAT USE BASIC EFFECTS

Usually an editor uses a *cut* to make the transition from one shot to another. However, many times the editor employs an *effect*, such as a dissolve, to make the transition from one shot to another. In this chapter we'll define these common effects and look at the creative ways filmmakers use them. Some of the effects are routine, some are inventive, some underscore the emotional intensity of a scene, and all must pass the test of serving the movie and advancing the story.

We'll start by repeating the cut shown at the beginning of Chapter 1. This way, you can clearly appreciate the difference between using a cut to make a transition and using an effect.

Using a cut (as opposed to an effect) to transition between two shots.

Pirates of the Caribbean: Dead Man's Chest

DISSOLVE

A transitional effect where the first (outgoing) shot disappears as the second (incoming) shot appears.

In this first shot, the mom-to-be prepares for the baby.

To understand how cuts and effects operate differently to transition from one shot to another, compare this dissolve to the cut on the opposite page.

Her shot (bottom frame) dissolves to another room in another house.

Then we see baby paraphernalia accumulating on the bed (right frame) as the pop-to-be (offscreen) also prepares.

Knocked Up

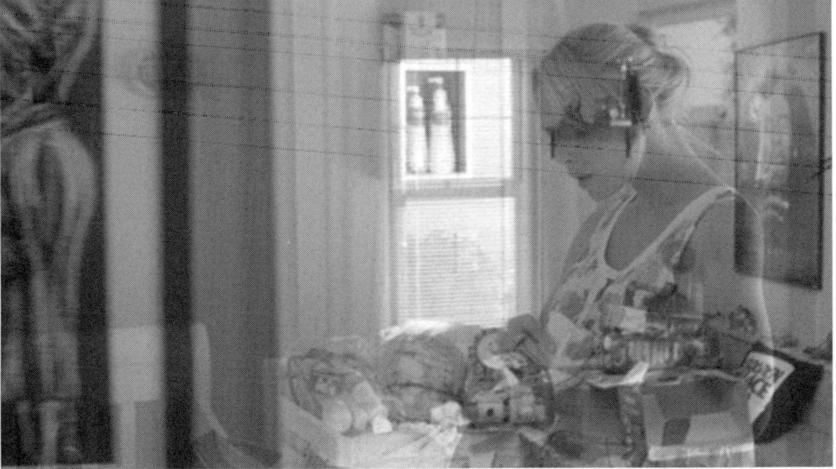

Dissolves typically portray the passage of time or a change in location or both as the dissolve from *Finding Neverland* illustrates. Regularly, dissolves are employed to eliminate jump cuts. They're also frequently combined with other effects, as we shall see later in this chapter.

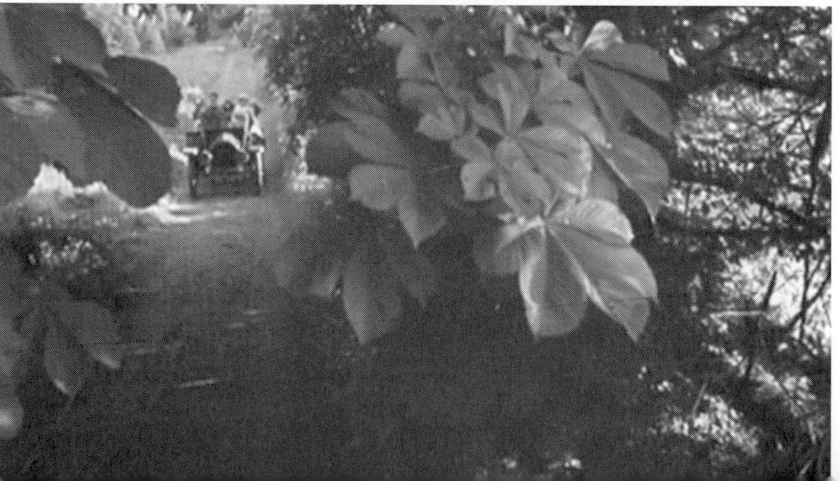

A trip from town to country and a change in tempo made possible by a desultory dissolve.

Finding Neverland

SHORT DISSOLVE:
Night becomes day
in the life of
a cartoon trucker.

Cars

Short dissolves quickly transport us to the next day and the next turn of the plot.

Long dissolves allow us to somberly reflect on the passing of time before being carried on.

LONG DISSOLVE: The years have not been kind to the town of Radiator Springs.

Cars

FADE IN AND FADE OUT

A fade is a dissolve to black, sometimes white, and once in awhile to yellow, blue, or another color. A fade in starts with black frames and dissolves to a filmed shot. A fade out does just the opposite; it dissolves from a filmed shot to black frames.

Many scenes and most movies begin with a fade in and end with a fade out. When placed in the body of a film, a fade out (usually paired with a fade in) often follows a scene of heartrending drama; the fades give the audience breathing space to absorb the emotion and be ready for what happens next.

FADE OUT: This scene takes on the look of a Renaissance painting with its fade to black as Sylvia Llewelyn Davies' life runs out.

Finding Neverland

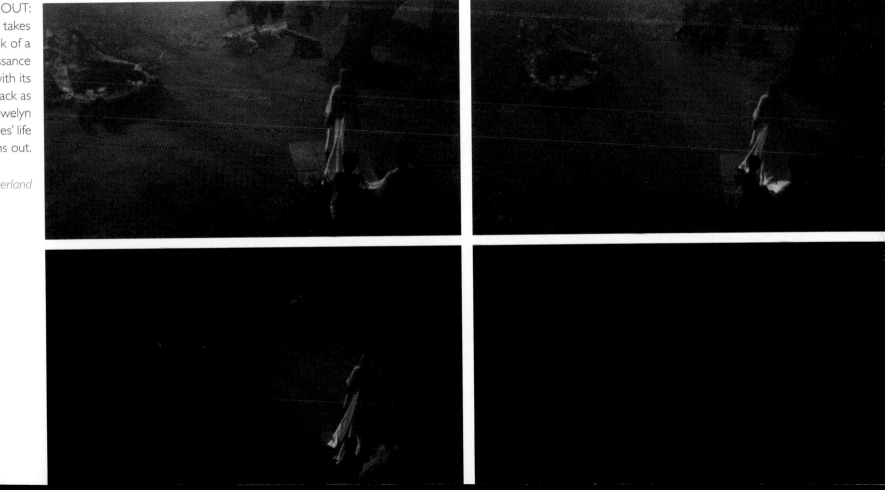

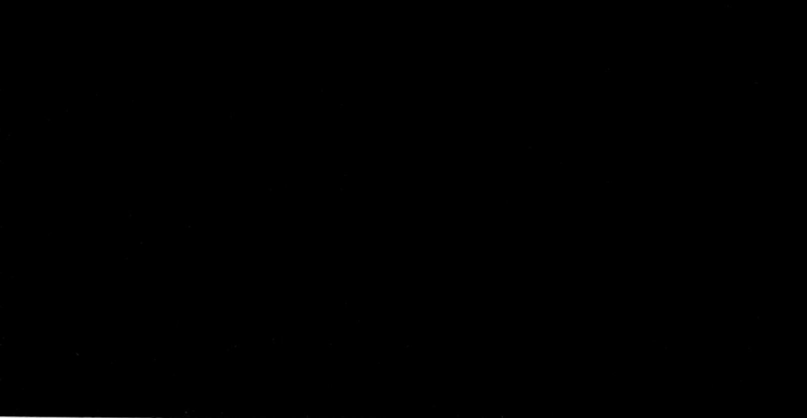

FADE IN:
The next scene fades in as people gather for Sylvia's funeral.

Finding Neverland

WHITE OUT

When a shot cuts or dissolves to white.

A white out often involves organic elements such as a light, a camera flashbulb, or steam. Along with black outs and fade outs, white outs are common devices for portraying death.

WHITE OUT 1: At the beginning of the movie, a white out uses the sun to bring Ofelia *from* her underground fantasy world *to* her real and dangerous world.

Pan's Labyrinth

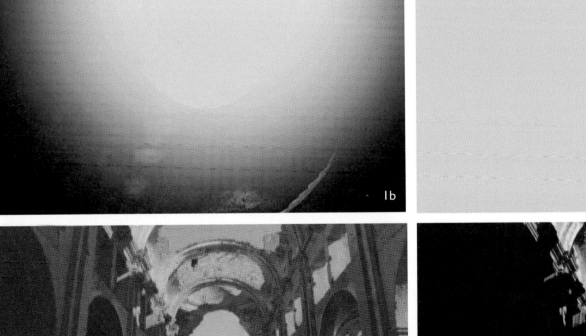

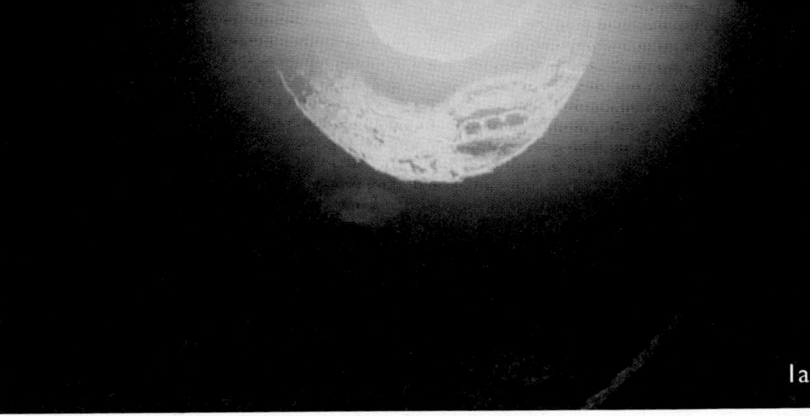

1a

1b

1c

She forgot who she was
and where she came from.

1d

She forgot who she was
and where she came from.

1e

WHITE OUT 2: Toward the end of the movie, an unusual white out uses the color yellow and repeats the sun imagery to take Ofelia *from* her death back *to* her fantasy world.

Pan's Labyrinth

WHITE OUT 3:
A shot of Ron whites out to a photo flash and reporter Rita Skeeter.

Harry Potter and the Goblet of Fire

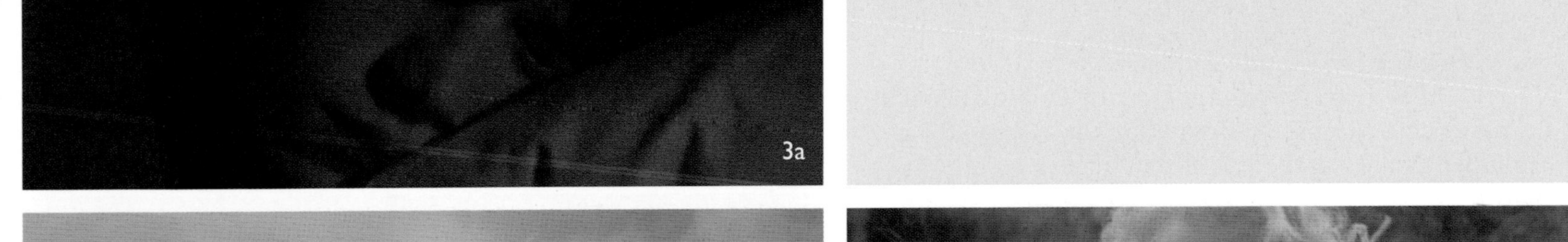

WHITE OUT 4:
A white out from the glare of an oncoming headlight is all in a day's work for an L.A. cop.

Crash

BLACK OUT

When a shot cuts (as opposed to employing a dissolve or other transitional effect) to black.

A black out is an abrupt and quite effective edit.

Cars begins with a series of cuts to black as a narrator describes the opening car race, setting the audience up for the rest of the movie.

1

2

3

4

5

FLASH FRAME

A frame of black or white inserted between two shots.

FLASH FRAME 1: This movie sizzles from beginning to end, sparked by white flash frames all the way. This one jumps the audience from Bourne's train to the CIA bureaucrat out to nail him.

The Bourne Ultimatum

The audience doesn't notice a flash frame but feels its power as it energizes the cut and zaps the action forward. Flash frames are often used to soften jump cuts, commonly in an interview with many cuts of the same person. White flash frames are also routinely used to simulate a camera flash and to extend a lightening flash.

FLASH FRAME 2: Here a black flash frame (frame 3), sandwiched in between one-frame dissolves (frames 2 and 4), brilliantly simulates how Jean-Do communicates with his only non-paralyzed part — his left eye. One blink — one black flash frame — means "oui"; two blinks — two black flash frames — means "non." And the answer to the question in the subtitle is (frame 3) "Oui."

The Diving Bell and the Butterfly

SUPER (SUPERIMPOSITION)

When two shots (or more) are held on top of each other full screen.

A super prolongs the value of each shot and intensifies the emotion of the moment. Supers are frequently used to reflect a character's state of mind.

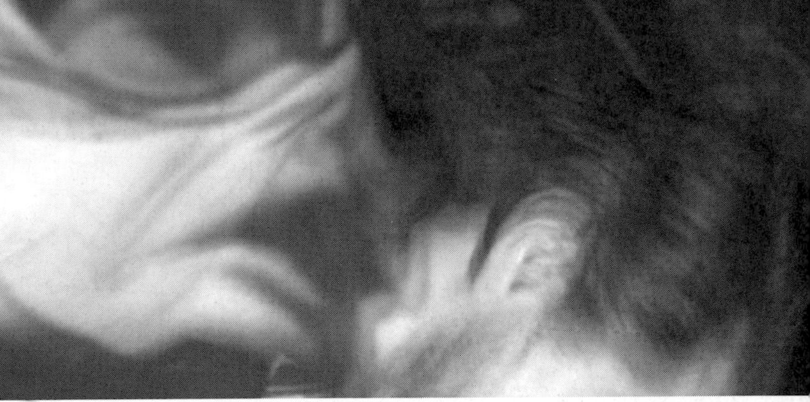

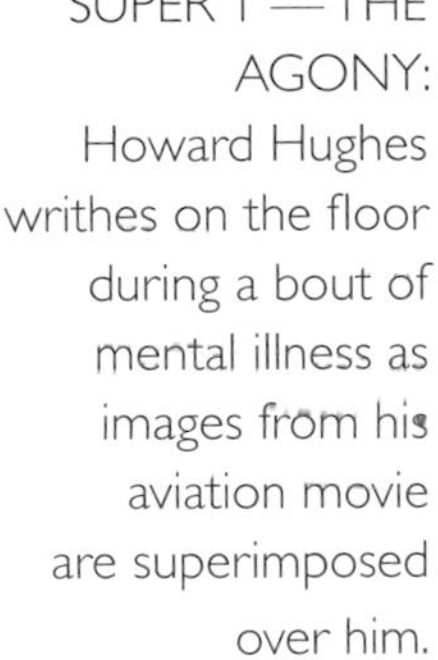

SUPER 1 — THE AGONY: Howard Hughes writhes on the floor during a bout of mental illness as images from his aviation movie are superimposed over him.

The Aviator

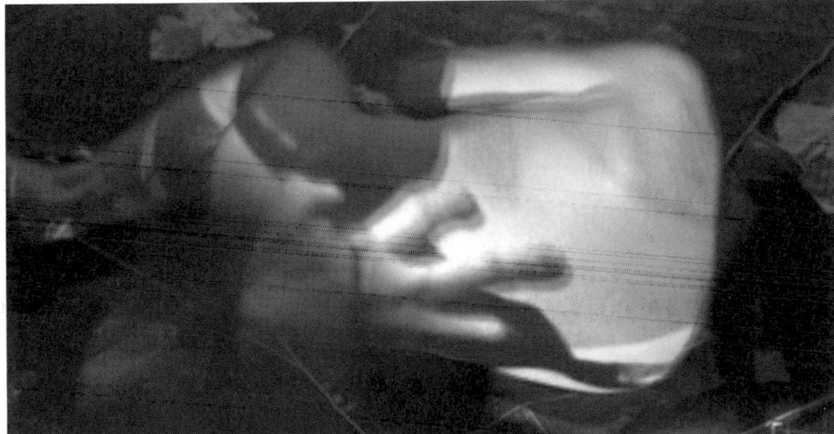

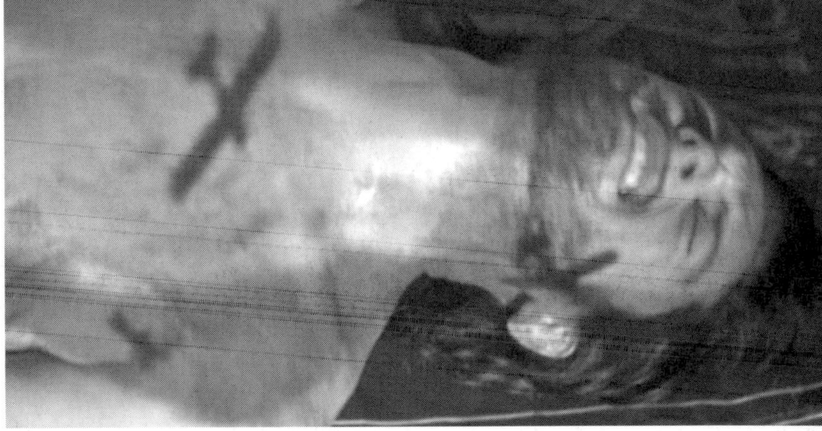

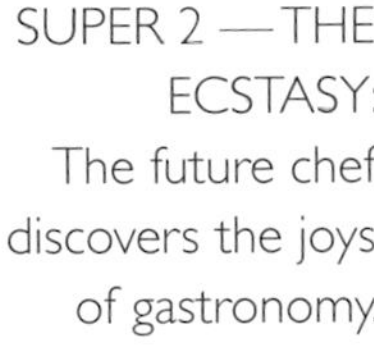

SUPER 2 — THE ECSTASY: The future chef discovers the joys of gastronomy.

Ratatouille

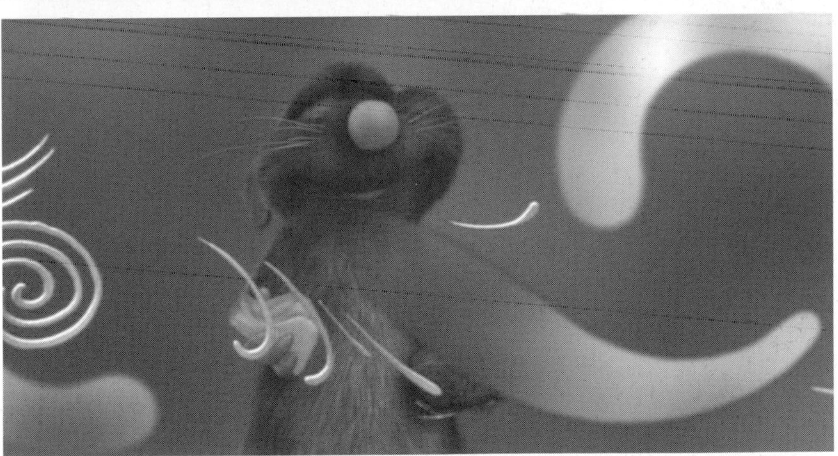

SUPER 3:
You can super (superimpose) a large, laughing enemy over your protagonists.

Paprika

SUPER 4:
Or you can super a friend or guru, a familiar ploy in both animated and non-animated movies. In this case the famous chef lectures the aspiring chef.

Ratatouille

Supers often incorporate windows to reflect a character's worries as supers 5-7 illustrate.

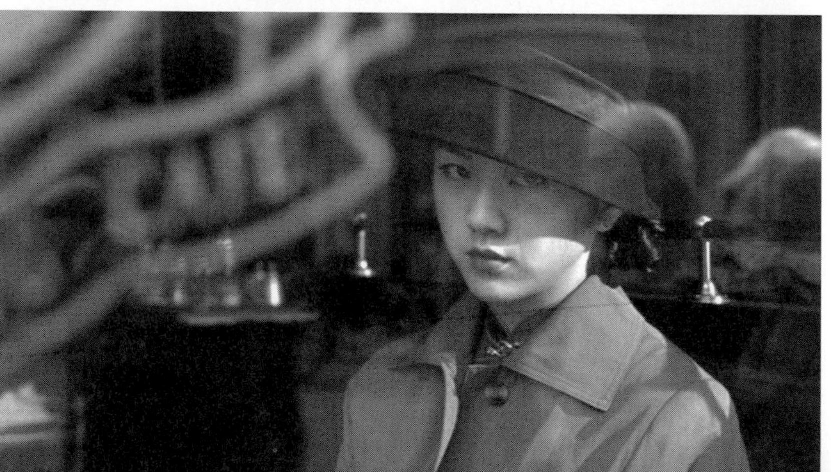

SUPER 5:
Passersby are supered over the main character as she contemplates a rendezvous crucial to her rebel gang's success.

Lust, Caution

SUPER 6:
A researcher frets as her co-worker undergoes surgery following an attack by their enemy.

Paprika

SUPER 7:
The Israeli counterterrorist leader looks out the plane's porthole (frame 1) and recalls the Munich massacre (frame 2), which bolsters his resolve to carry out the team's next assassination.

Munich

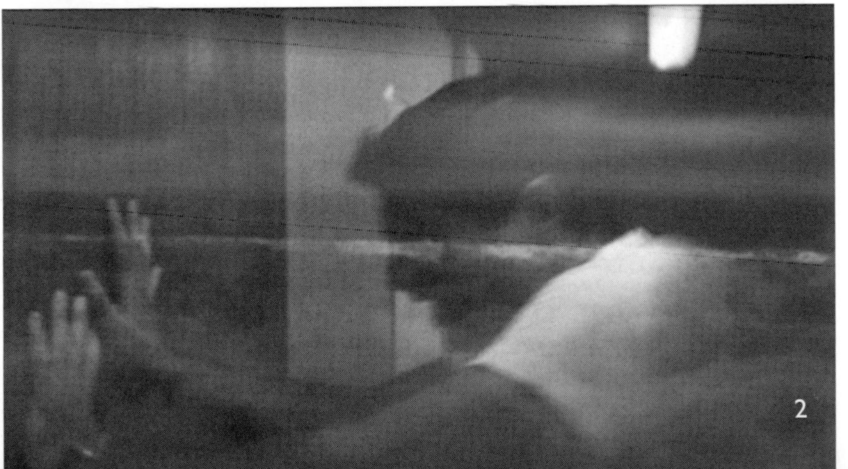

Supers can also portray a character's memories, fears, or adventures as seen in Supers 8-10.

SUPER 8:
A collage of superimposed images composes a scrapbook of Jean-Do's past.

The Diving Bell and the Butterfly

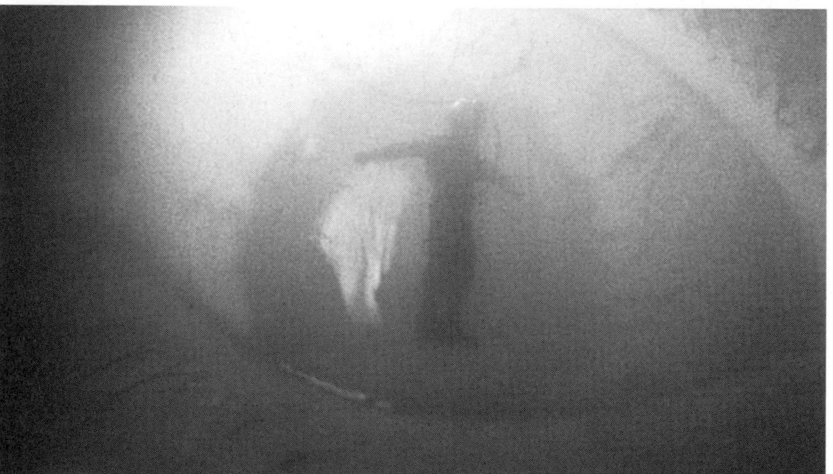

SUPER 9:
Jean-Do's metaphor for his paralyzed condition — a man imprisoned in a diving bell — is depicted by a superimposition.

The Diving Bell and the Butterfly

SUPER 10:
A kaleidoscope of supers accompanies the pair of investigators as they make their way across London.

The Da Vinci Code

SUPER 11:

Paprika

SUPER 12:

Spider-Man 2

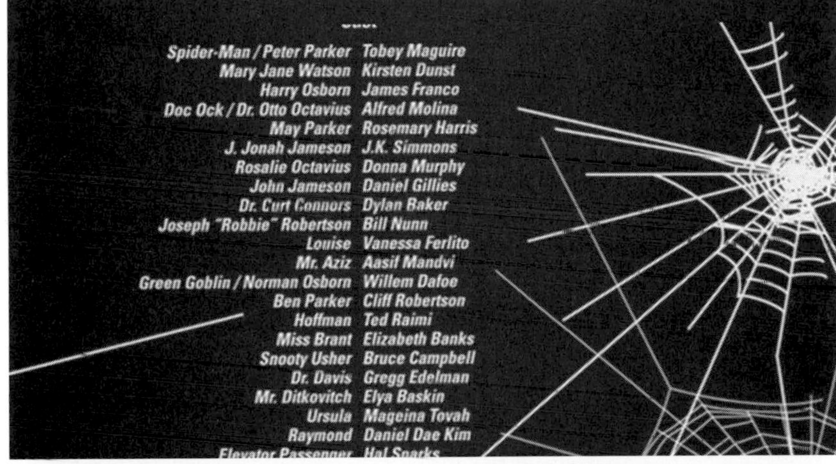

SUPER 13:

Brokeback Mountain

Lastly, movie titles and credits constitute superimpositions and are placed over a variety of backgrounds such as animations, black frames, live action footage, or freeze frames.

WRAP UP

Now that you've got the hang of basic effects, we'll look at effects that are complex and require more time, thought, and money to manufacture. Use these only if they fit your project and you have the software and the budget!

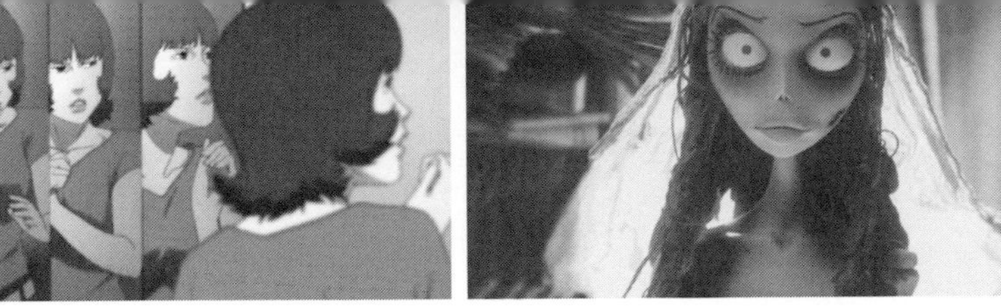

chapter 5 CUTS THAT USE COMPLEX EFFECTS

We live in an era where hardly a movie appears that doesn't exhibit some sort of special effect; many blockbusters depend on novel effects to bolster their appeal. Effects can take days, weeks, or months to craft on the computer and in the film lab. Then they are cut into the movie by the editor and finalized during the finishing process that takes place after the editor turns in the final cut of the show.

There are many fine books on how these effects are created. Since this book is about the types of cuts editors make to put one shot after another into a movie, we'll focus on the complex effects editors routinely influence by either selecting the footage, helping with design, or knocking out the initial version on their digital editing system.

WIPE

A transitional effect where the incoming shot replaces the outgoing shot by appearing to push (wipe) it from the screen. A wipe literally pushes the action forward from one shot to the next.

Wipes are a basic effect with an endless variety of patterns, which is why they're included under complex effects. A wipe can draw attention to itself and act as a clear marker of change, or be subtle due to its speed or inventive use of elements.

WIPE 1: Charging soldiers wipe to Ofelia strolling amongst the ferns. A vertical brown stripe, appearing to be a tree, forms the edge of this horizontal wipe.

Pan's Labyrinth

A wipe can move horizontally — starting from the left or right — and imitate a camera pan. Or a wipe can travel vertically — up or down — and imitate a camera tilt. *Note*: Wipes composed on digital editing systems can start anywhere — for example, from one corner of the frame or all four — and move in any direction.

WIPE 2:
A sign moves from the bottom to the top of the frame to create this vertical wipe from theatre to Western set.

Finding Neverland

Wipes, like dissolves, are often used to bridge scenes or to signify the passage of time. Also, like dissolves, wipes frequently start from black or include black frames.

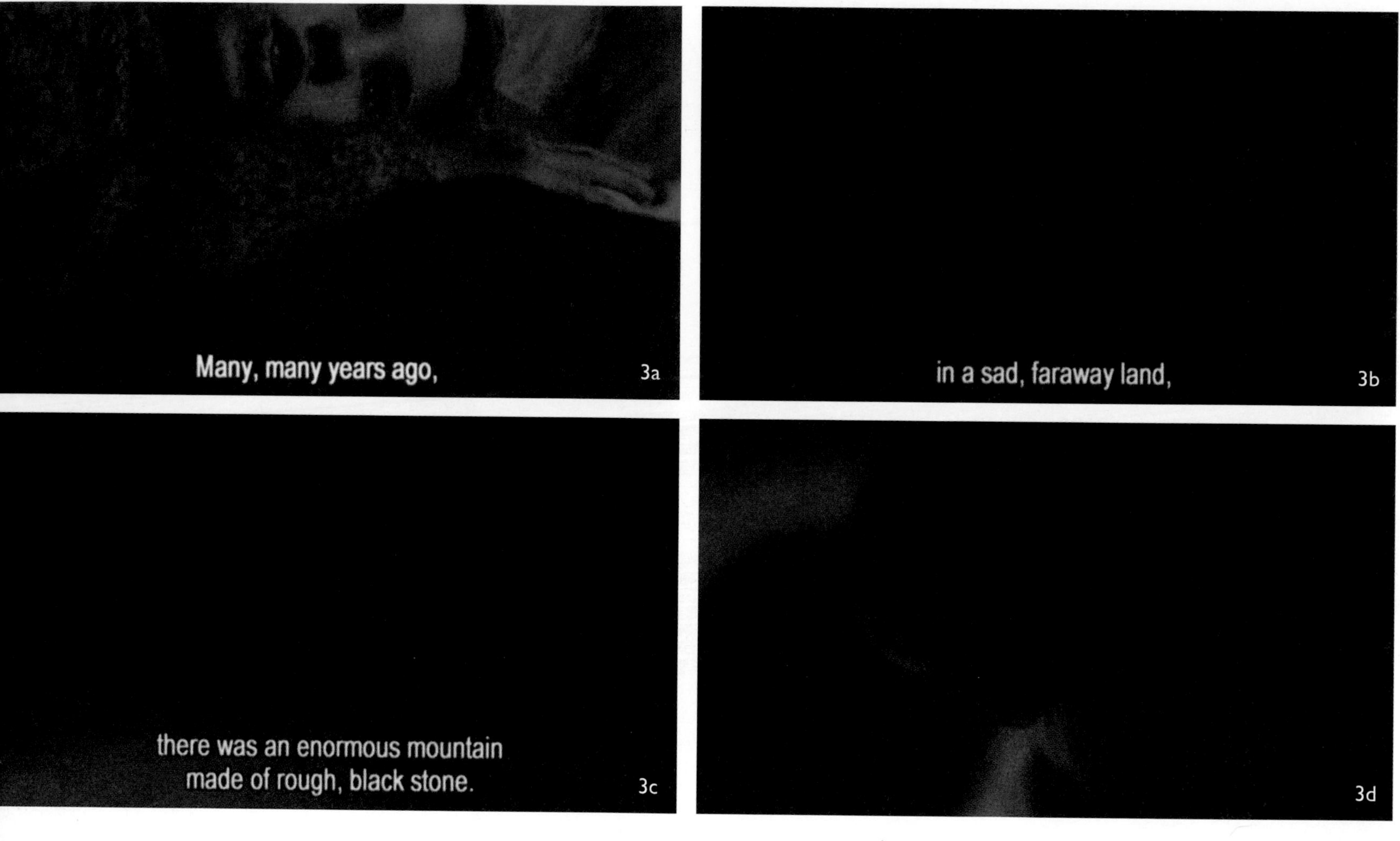

Many, many years ago,
3a
in a sad, faraway land,
3b
there was an enormous mountain
made of rough, black stone.
3c
3d

WIPE 3:
This vertical wipe crosses time, space, and color — from the eerie blue of the outer world to the blood orange of the womb.

Pan's Labyrinth

A wipe can be an intrinsic part of the composition of a shot — a door opening, a car swooshing by, a curtain rising or falling — all repeatedly work as wipes between shots.

WIPE 4: This "barn door" wipe uses the courthouse doors to send the action from the exterior to the interior of the courthouse.

Cars

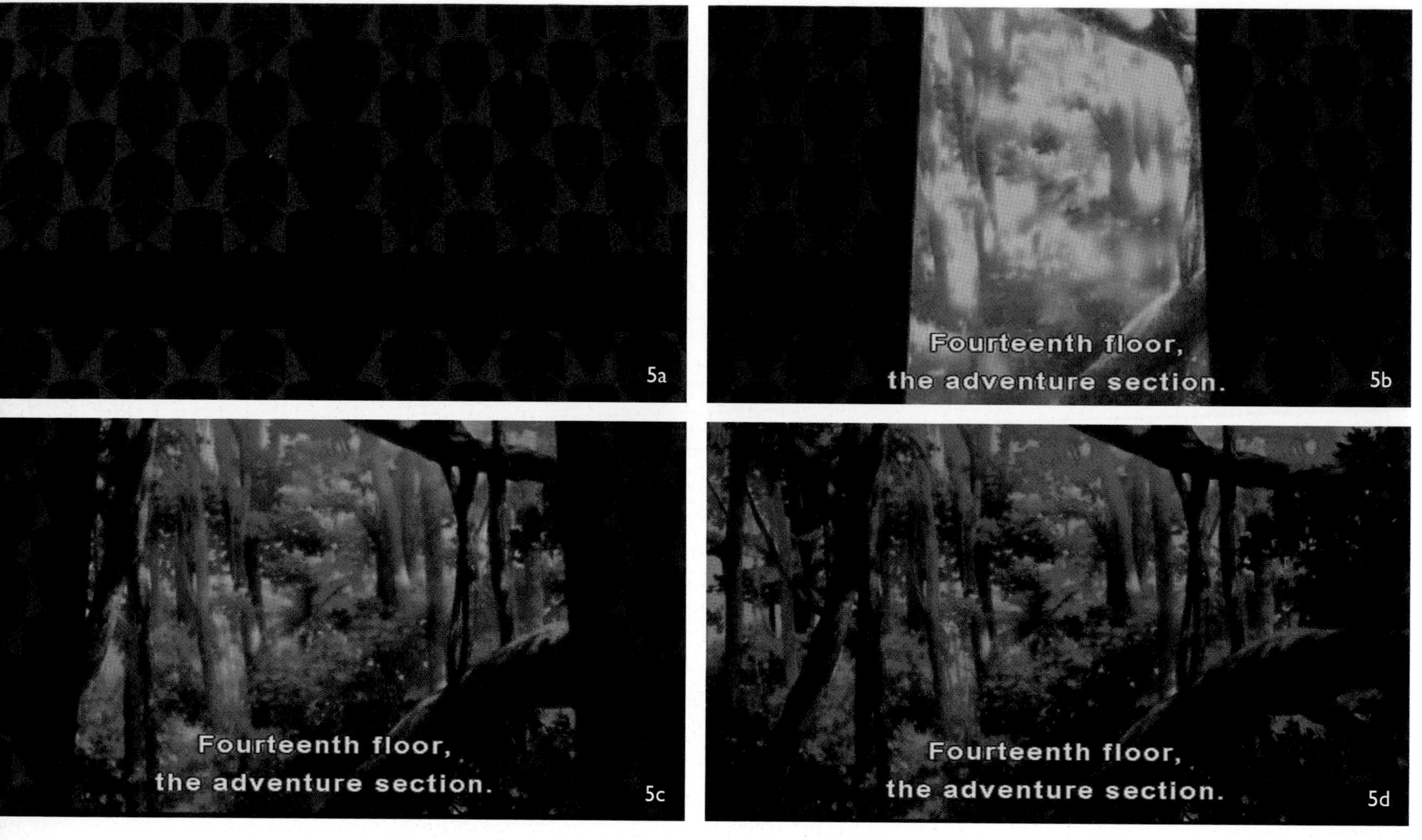

WIPE 5:
In this magical scene, department store elevator doors open in a wipe that takes viewers outside to the forest.

Paprika

Besides doors, cars, and curtains, many other innate elements in shots are used as wipes: Passersby and elements of nature are a couple of prime examples.

WIPE 6:
A bicyclist wipes the screen (middle frame), wheeling the audience from the heroine in the café (top frame) to the object of her glance (bottom frame).

Lust, Caution

WIPE 7:
The undercarriage of a train (middle frame) transports the scene from a wide shot of cowboy to a medium shot of him having a smoke.

Brokeback Mountain

WIPE 8:
A wave laps the screen to carry the main character from beach to sea.

There Will Be Blood

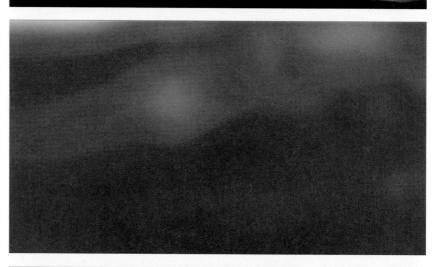

These two last pages of wipes highlight their variety and the witty originality of Tim Burton, director of *Corpse Bride*.

WIPE 9:
Birds flock, creating a wipe that sucks the groom away from his beloved betrothed on the balcony to his accidental corpse bride in the underworld.

Corpse Bride

WIPE 10:
In the first shot (frames 10 a,b,c), the hero backs away from the crowd and toward camera, wiping the screen with his rear end. In the second shot (frames 10 d,e,f), he turns and retreats from camera and toward a new crowd — minus the corpse bride.

Corpse Bride

GREENSCREEN (A.K.A. BLUE SCREEN)

Creating a new shot by compositing (merging) two shots together.

GREENSCREEN 1: Sword fighters greenscreened separately against a forest and lake background.

Hero

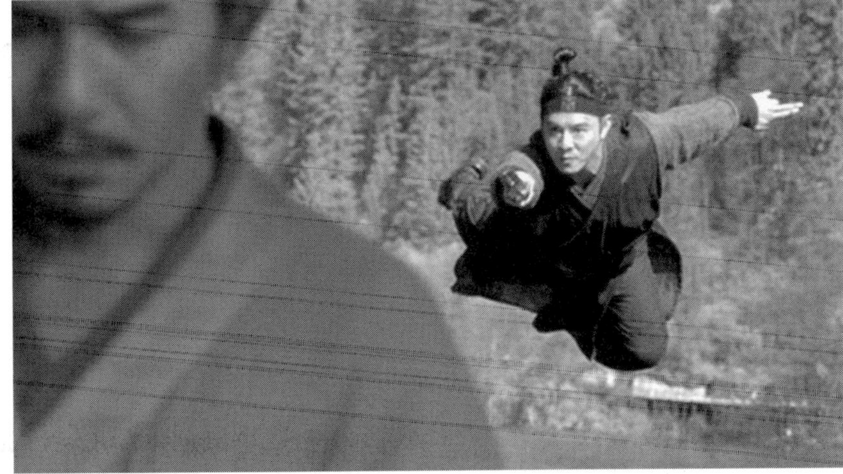

Shot 1, a live action shot, makes up the background. *Example*: A forested lake.

Shot 2, the greenscreen shot, makes up the foreground. It's created by filming the subject performing in front of a green (or blue) screen.
Example: A sword fighter lunges at his opponent.

When the two shots are composited, the greenscreen washes out and the subject appears to react to what's happening in the background live action shot.
Example: Now the sword fighter appears to be lunging across the lake.

Greenscreen is used to broadcast weather reports and has become a staple effect in movies. A simple greenscreen can be composed by the editor on a digital system; more complicated greenscreens are created by a special effects house or film lab. Audiences have grown accustomed to seeing these and other complex composited shots — they're the stuff of effects makers' imaginations and hard work.

What is the greenscreen shot in each of these examples? You figure it out. Hint: It's the foreground shot.

GREENSCREEN 2: Spidey at home with his girlfriend.

Spider-Man 2

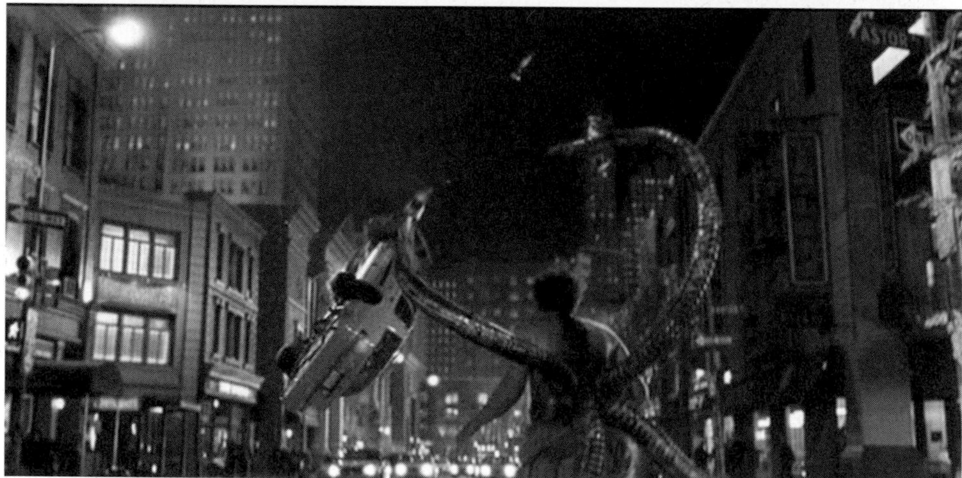

GREENSCREEN 3: Villain Doc Ock give a New York City cab the heave ho.

Spider-Man 2

MATTE (A.K.A. KEY)

Creating a hole in a shot and placing (keying) another shot in that hole.

MATTE 1-3: Alex Supertramp (the name Chris McCandless, the subject of this bi-opic, gave himself), adventures across North America (frames 1 and 2) while his parents bicker and fret back in Virginia (frame 3).

Into the Wild

As with split frame shots, the audience amasses knowledge at a more rapid rate when matte shots are used. The editor selects the shots to be matted, although the actual matting may be done at the film lab or postproduction facility (places where all picture and sound elements are brought together and finalized).

Matte 4 contains an inset, an effect where a reduced shot is placed on another shot. Typically, an inset highlights a detail of the main shot.

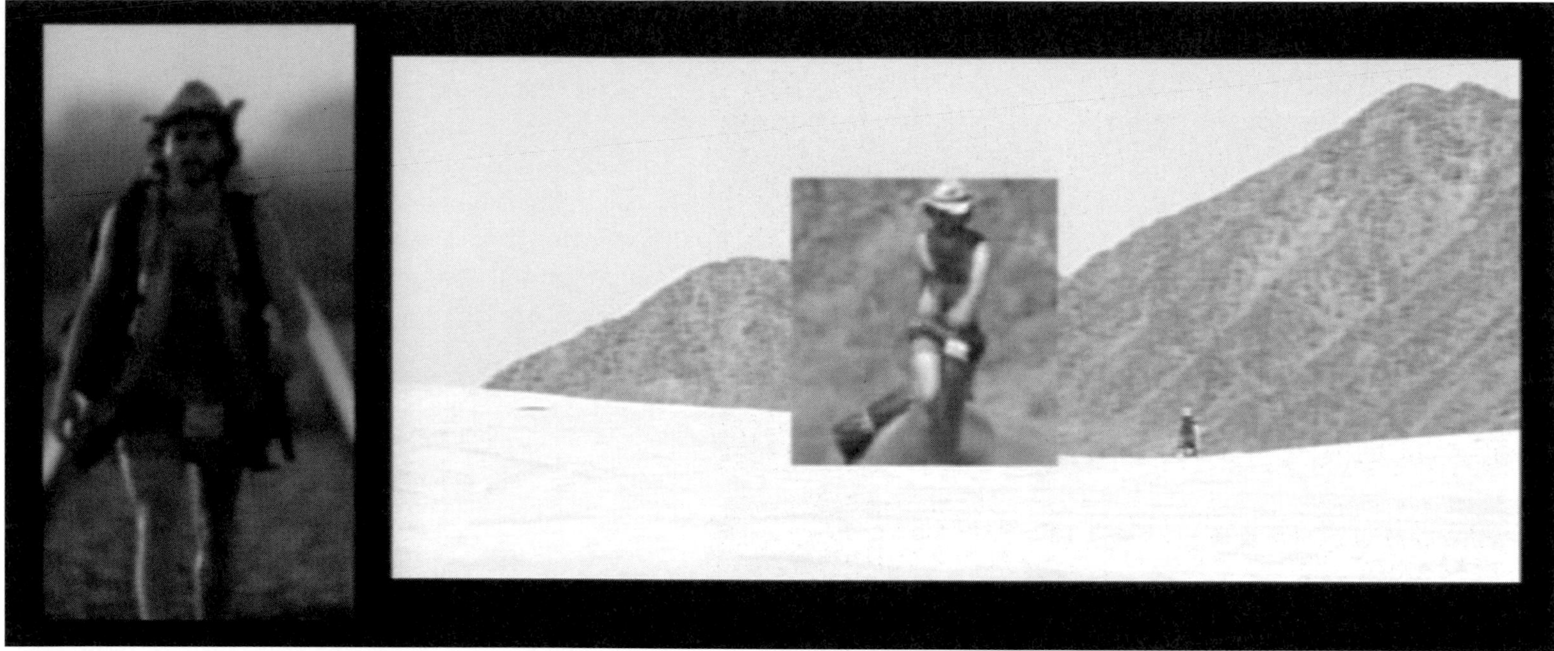

MATTE 4:
Alex Supertramp backpacks (left matte) and tows his kayak through Baja California (right matte). The inset in the middle of the right-hand matte shows the towing in greater detail.

Into the Wild

Television sets routinely function as mattes.

MATTE 5:
A matte shot, cut into a TV, broadcasts original news footage of the 1972 Munich massacre.

Munich

MATTE 6:
The big race is matted into the press room monitor.

Cars

Windows are also perfect, commonly used mattes.

MATTE 7: The kitchen door porthole provides a matte for a shot that centers on the all-important food critic.

Ratatouille

MATTE 8: Travelling toward Hogwarts school for wizards, the scenery is matted in through the train window.

Harry Potter and the Goblet of Fire

A matte can be any shape — rectangular, round, keyhole — the list goes on.

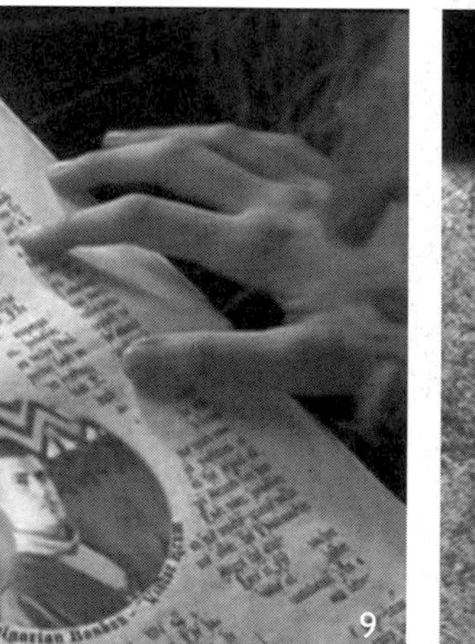

MATTE 9:
The Daily Prophet features live news coverage embedded in a heart-shaped and a round matte.

Harry Potter and the Goblet of Fire

MATTE 10:
A softly focused newspaper serves as a matte for this POV shot.

Finding Neverland

MATTE 11:
Can you spot the mattes in this shot? Yep! It's the paintings: Their frames are mattes and their subjects react along with the student wizards.

Harry Potter and the Goblet of Fire

MATTE 12:
Here a car's rear view mirror makes a perfect matte.

No Country for Old Men

MATTE 13:
In this unique shot, each sliver of mirror is a matte reflecting Paprika's reactions to a repugnant remark.

Paprika

SPLIT SCREEN

Dividing the screen into two or more parts with different shots in each division.

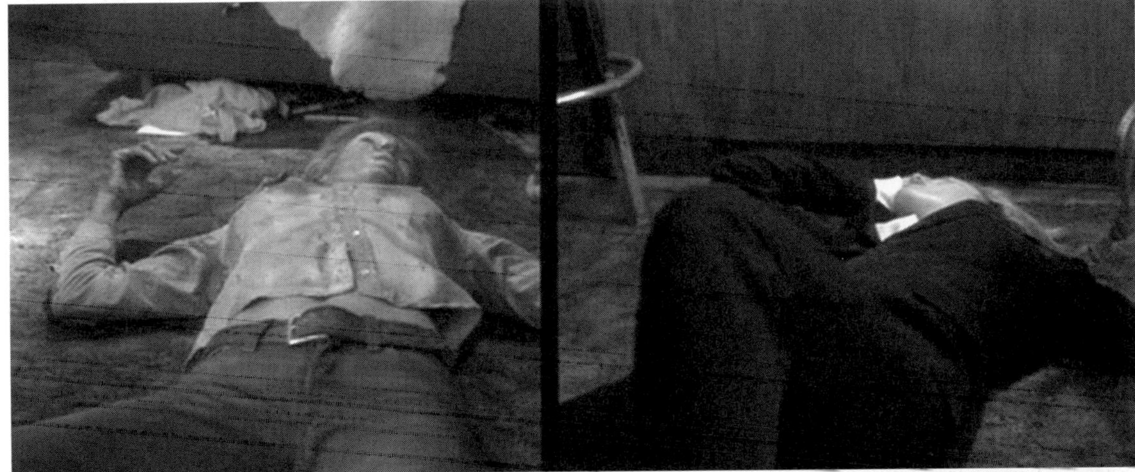

SPLIT SCREEN 1: The Bride (left) and her enemy take a breather during their punishing fight.

Kill Bill: Vol. 2

SPLIT SCREEN 2: Foraging and starvation — two sides of the survival theme of this movie — are brought together in a split screen frame.

Into the Wild

Split screens came in vogue with the movie *Woodstock* in 1970 and have been regularly seen on tube and screen ever since. A split screen can project several different shots or show the same action from slightly different perspectives. Either way, the editor selects the shots and their duration and the audience takes in more information and usually, more meaning from the doubling up of shots.

SPLIT SCREEN 3: Converging walls form the split screen effect in this scene between a mentally ill Howard Hughes (left) and Pan Am president Juan Trippe.

The Aviator

SPLIT SCREEN 4: Fire splits the shots of Howard Hughes (right) and his CEO.

The Aviator

A split screen can also convey relation, excitement, and frenzy; a multi-split screen bombards the audience with images.

SPLIT SCREEN 5: Two-way and four-way split screens capture surgeons fending off a patient run amok — Doc Ock.

Spider-Man 2

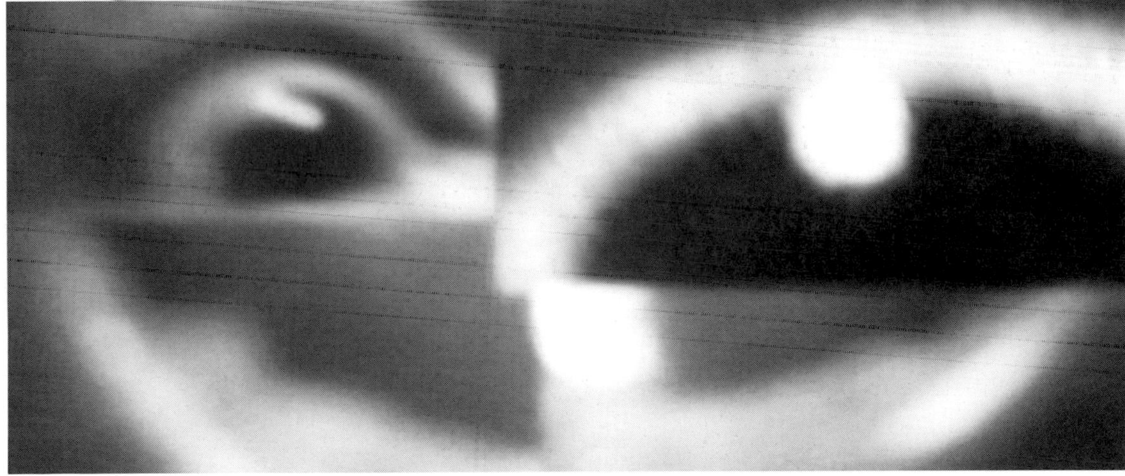

WRAP UP

As you've seen, special effects can be extremely inventive and complex and make for intricate, spellbinding storytelling. We've just grazed the surface here — whole careers are forged in creating everyday and extraordinary effects — but hopefully you have a better appreciation of what is possible.

In the next chapter, for a complete change of pace, we'll talk about… pace. Along with rhythm and time, pace is critical to holding viewers' interest: Successful editing depends on all three of these elements. The next chapter provides prime examples of the power of properly paced editing.

chapter 6 CUTTING FOR PACE, RHYTHM, AND TIME

The rhythm of the editing plays a vital role in every film. Why? Because rhythm corrals all the elements — performance, cinematography, sound, and story — to define the rate at which the audience receives information. It is the pulse that infuses the show into the audience's psyche.

So how does rhythm relate to pace? Pace is the speed at which the cuts go by. More precisely, it's the duration of cuts and the number of cuts in a sequence, e.g. short and many or long and few. Rhythm results from pacing and bringing all the elements together — it is *how* the edited sequence plays. We're aware of it in the midst of a pounding action scene or shortly thereafter when we let out our breath in the more slowly paced aftermath scene.

Rhythm in editing is similar to rhythm in music. Indeed the terms are the same: rhythm, pace, sequence. A movie's rhythm and pacing are often accented or driven by music or sounds. In editing, as with music, there are fast, medium, and slow sequences as well as abrupt actions that catch viewers off guard and pauses that give them a respite from the action.

Filmmaker Andrei Tarkovsky claimed, in his book *Sculpting in Time*, "What is different about cinema editing is that it brings together time, imprinted in the segments of film."

How do pace and rhythm relate to time? Shots enter the cutting room, each with its own timing created by the duration of the filmed action. The editor takes these shots and uses parts of them to pace and sculpt the movie, creating a new timing and the movie's rhythm. Editing shortens or lengthens the real time of the filmed action, causing time to be compressed or expanded.

In this chapter we'll examine cuts and sequences to pinpoint how time, pace, and rhythm reveal character, support the dramatic action, and affect the audience.

COMPRESSING TIME *Editing to contract real time.*

A time-compressed sequence conveys information swiftly. Typically, it brings high energy or chaos to the screen and startles, scares, or otherwise socks it to the audience. Dialogue, sound effects, and music often punctuate these sequences, overlapping cuts and sustaining continuity.

Editors compress time in a number of ways including: making cuts that are short in duration (2" or less), employing dissolves, mattes, or other effects, and creating a fast pace.

COMPRESSING TIME 1 (selected cuts): In this opening sequence, horses hurtle across ancient China to rush the nameless hero (inside the coach) toward the emperor.

Hero

Long journeys are edited to compress real time as well as to efficiently convey story points and provide a sense of place and time period.

I was orphaned at a young age
and was never given a name.

Short journeys, such as a character crossing a room or moving from one place to another, are habitually edited to avoid tedium. The result? Time is compressed.

COMPRESSING TIME 2 (selected cuts): The hero's final walk to the Emperor's palace takes a thousand steps and three cuts.

Hero

Time compression is frequently used to show growth, change, or shape shifting such as a character turning into a werewolf.

COMPRESSING TIME 3 (selected cuts): A running researcher changes into Paprika, her alter ego, via time-compressing cuts.

Paprika

When a time-compressed sequence is an action scene, close-ups and medium shots comprise the majority of shots because viewers grasp their information faster than that from long or wide shots. As the action sequence accelerates toward its climax, the cuts usually become even shorter and the rhythm rapid-fire.

COMPRESSING TIME 4 (selected cuts): In 43 seconds and 36 cuts, pilot Howard Hughes goes down in flames.

The Aviator

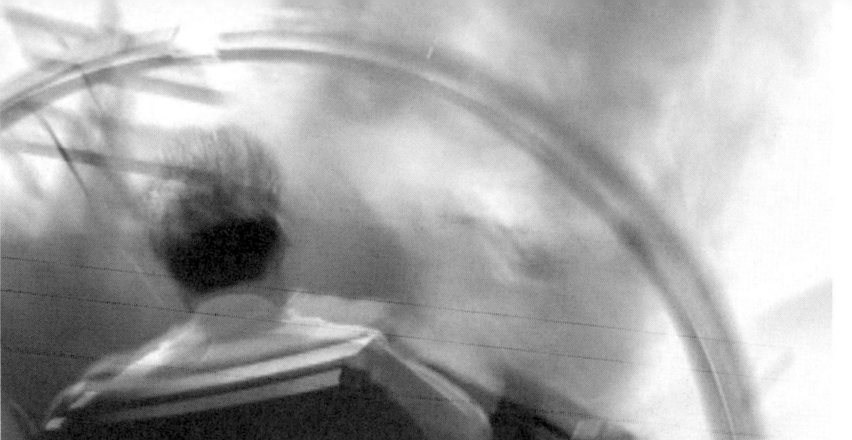
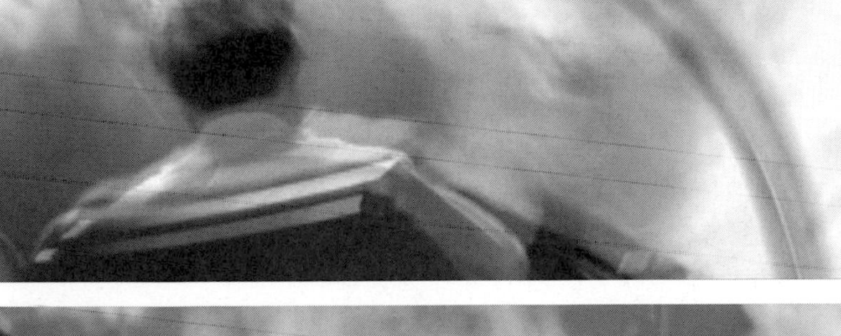

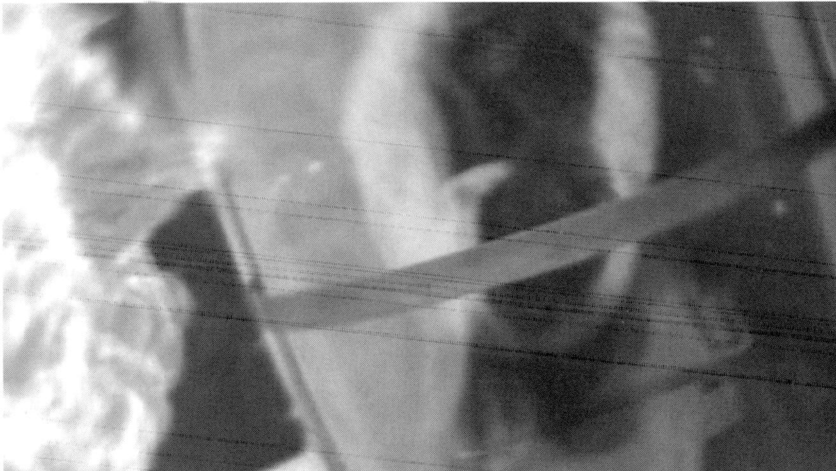
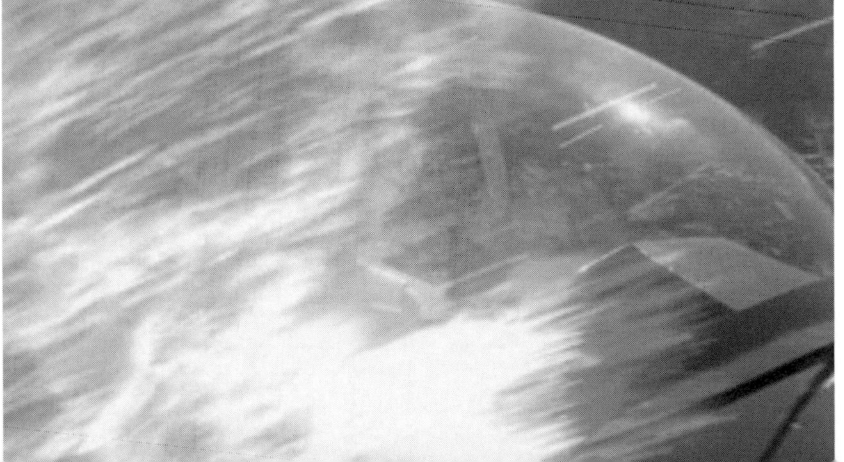

SMASH CUT

Variation on a short cut. An unexpected, lightning-quick cut designed to deliberately jar the audience by zapping the action from one place/ object/person/image to another.

SMASH CUT 1:
An Iraqi girl's carefree slide ends in the kaboom of the U.S. attack.

Fahrenheit 911

SMASH CUT 2: Budd, is not counting on this fatal payoff. He's as shocked as the audience.

Kill Bill: Vol. 2

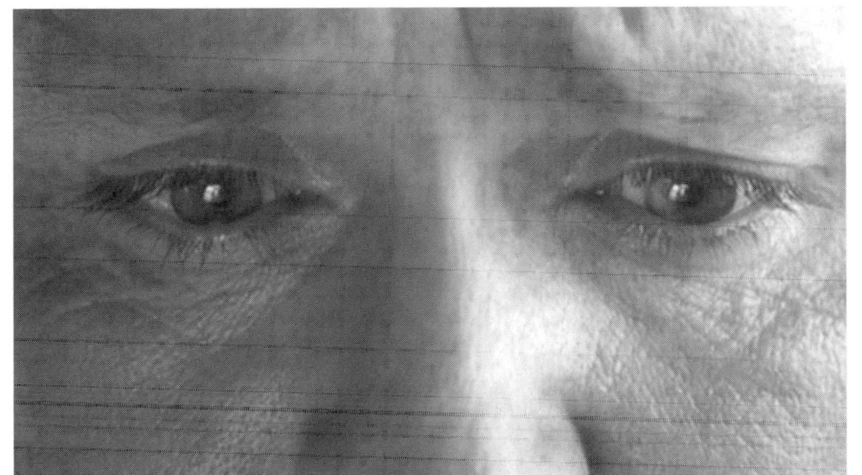

SMASH CUT 3: An alien pops into frame through a screen.

War of the Worlds

Sometimes smash cuts are literal smashes.

SMASH CUT 4: The eye-patched villain is surprised by The Bride, who smash cuts feet first through a wall to attack her.

Kill Bill: Vol. 2

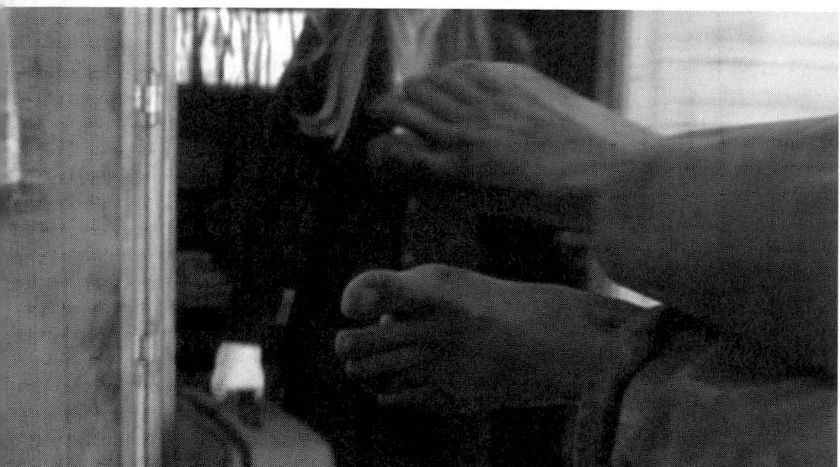

SMASH CUT 5: The hunted serial killer finds himself in more trouble when a station wagon (right) suddenly appears and crashes into his car.

No Country for Old Men

EXPANDING TIME

Editing to lengthen real time.

Editors expand time in a variety of instances. For example, they stretch time to show two people embracing or fighting, to extend a comic moment, or to call out an athlete executing an awesome move. This elongates the moment, like a sustained note or repeated phrase in music, and lets viewers fully experience the emotion and what's taking place.

Time is expanded by editors in many ways such as: cutting in multiple angles of an action, using cuts that are long in duration, and editing in a slow or medium rhythm.

EXPANDING TIME 1 (selected cuts): Repeated action of crossbow soldiers stretch time before the battle begins.

Hero

EXPANDING TIME 2: An exhilarating jump of freedom is extended by cuts to multiple angles.

Into the Wild

STOPPING TIME

A variation on expanding time where the editing causes a pause in the action, appearing to stop time.

STOPPING TIME 1: During a pull back in battle, the captain exhorts his lieutenant, Serrano, and consults his pocket watch.

Pan's Labyrinth

Go ahead, Serrano, don't be afraid,
this is the only decent way to die.

Ordinarily, time-stopping edits are accomplished through reaction shots or POV shots held on screen. Like a rest in music, these edits are usually seen prior to a climax and function to re-focus the audience on what's at stake and the possible outcomes. Prime examples include courtroom scenes before the verdict is delivered and sports competitions before the winning putt, hit, or shot clinches the event.

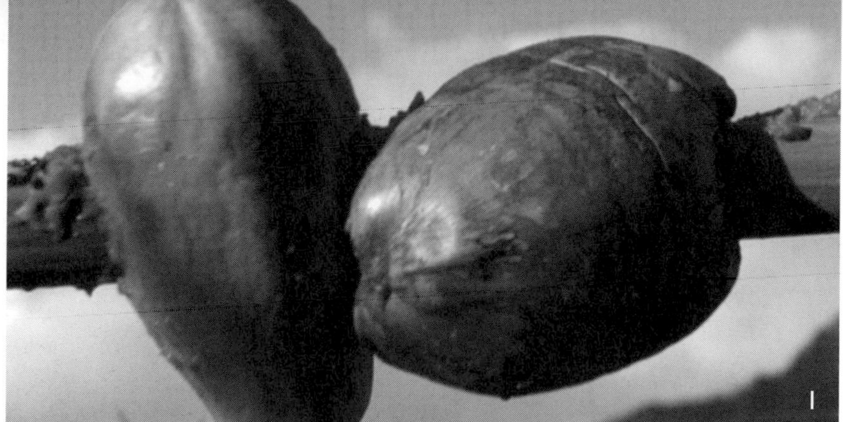

STOPPING TIME 2 (selected shots): Peeved at being pelted with papayas, pirate Jack Sparrow shouts "Stop it!" (frames 1-3).

Pirates of the Caribbean: Dead Man's Chest

STOPPING TIME 2 (continued): The action halts (frames 4-6) and Jack winks at the audience (frame 7) before the action restarts.

Pirates of the Caribbean: Dead Man's Chest

SUBJECTIVE TIME

Cutting to show time experienced from a character's point of view.

Film is considered to be the art that most mimics the human mind. Both mind and movie can dart from thought to feeling, knowledge to discovery, past to present in a nanosecond. Editing from a character's point of view exemplifies this and is what allows film to cross into and mesh with our own lives — our dreams, hopes, fears, beliefs, and experiences.

1a

1b

1c

1d

SUBJECTIVE TIME 1: Days of marching through the desert without food and water increase The Bride's thirst for revenge.

Kill Bill: Vol. 2

SUBJECTIVE TIME 2 (selected cuts): Roaming the streets of downtown Los Angeles cements Alex's decision to head for the wilds of Alaska. Director Sean Penn used the same actor for two different characters so Alex Supertramp (bottom right) literally pictures himself as just another phony urbanite (bottom left).

Into the Wild

FLASH CUT

A combination of subjective time and compressed time: Short cut that quickly and intensively gets inside a character's head.

Flash cuts sear the audience's brain with what a character is seeing and feeling. While editing *The Pawnbroker* in 1962, director Sidney Lumet and editor Ralph Rosenblum pioneered the use of flash cuts in the U.S. Rosenblum described their vision in his book, *When the Shooting Stops…The Editing Begins*: "They [flash cuts] would represent the beginnings of a memory voyage, the mind's instantaneous, semiconscious, involuntary association of current and past events." Their vision has proved true as the next three examples illustrate.

FLASH CUT 1 (selected cuts): When Howard Hughes arrives at a movie premiere, the sight and sound of flashbulbs assault him, exposing one of his many phobias.

The Aviator

FLASH CUT 2
(selected cuts):
City life strobes
at him in flash cuts
as Paprika's
detective friend
has a heart attack.

Paprika

FLASH CUT 3 (selected cuts): Death scene of Chris (a.k.a. Alex Supertramp). Flash cuts of the sky outside his window and an imagined reconciliation with his parents, accompany Chris to his death in the final frame.

Into the Wild

3g

3h

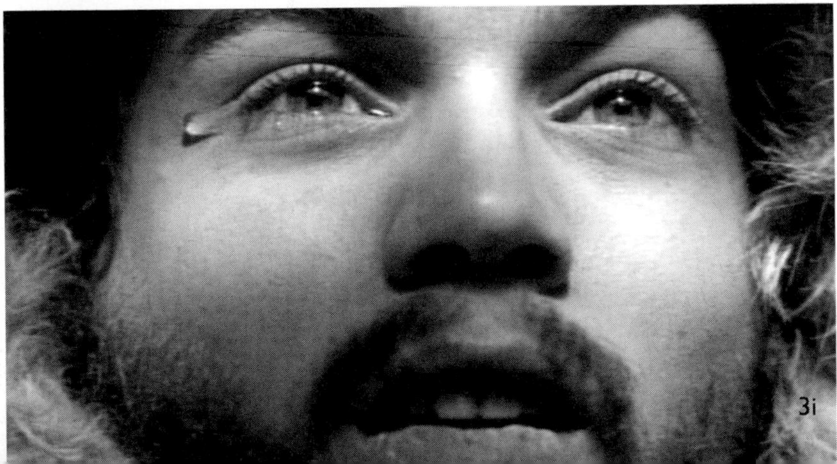
3i

SUBLIMINAL CUT

A cut consisting of a few frames which zip by so fast that the viewer is only subliminally (subconsciously) aware of them.

In the mid-1950s a market researcher announced that he'd increased snack counter sales by inserting subliminal cuts into a movie, urging the audience to buy popcorn and drink Coca Cola. Ever since, the public has worried about being manipulated by subliminal advertising in movies as well as on television, billboards, radio, and other recording media.

But do subliminal cuts really stimulate us to buy products? Do self-help recordings played while we're half-conscious or asleep improve our knowledge? Even though the FCC banned subliminal cuts in the 1970s following congressional hearings, there has been no conclusive scientific evidence that subliminal messages increase our knowledge or stimulate us to change our normal behavior. And the market researcher eventually admitted that he faked not only the results but the movie theatre experiment itself — it never happened.

So — do movies contain subliminal cuts? Absolutely. How do they impact the audience? Like any other good cut, they serve the story. The shortest of all cuts, a subliminal cut can ratchet up the tension to help make the audience uneasy. Additionally, it can expose the past, foreshadow the future, or show what a character is experiencing.

Here's what director William Friedkin said in 1973 about why he put subliminal cuts in *The Exorcist*: "The subliminal cut is the single most provocative and useful tool that a filmmaker has today as a story-telling device because it really expresses the way all of us think in cinematic terms: The way when we're walking down the street or talking to each other and while you're looking at me, or I at you, we're flashing on something else constantly. The way the mind reaches into God-knows-where for a picture out of our subconscious."

For such a small cut it certainly has had a lot said and written about it! Let's look a few subliminal cuts and you can decide what you think.

SUBLIMINAL CUT 1: As he is chased in a dark-lit scene, Bourne's past intercepts him in a series of brightly lit subliminal cuts.

The Bourne Ultimatum

Subliminal cuts, flash frames, and flash cuts contribute mightily to these two high-energy films — the first a thriller, the second a comedy.

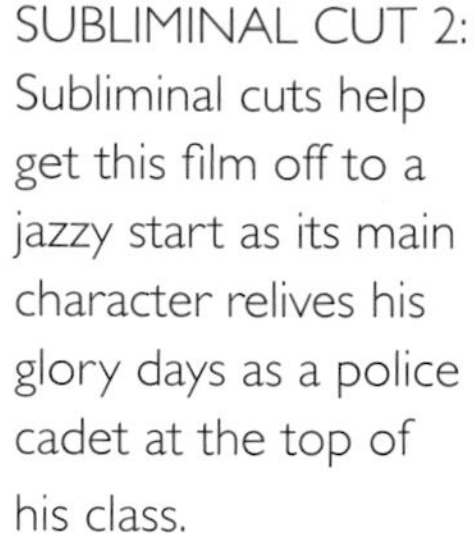

SUBLIMINAL CUT 2: Subliminal cuts help get this film off to a jazzy start as its main character relives his glory days as a police cadet at the top of his class.

Hot Fuzz

UNIVERSAL TIME *Cutting to invoke the universal relevance of a time, place, or idea.*

The opposite of subliminal cuts, universal time cuts are typically slow and deliberate, giving the audience time to breathe in their message.

The Diving Bell and the Butterfly ends with Jean-Do's death, followed by a sequence of glaciers reconstituting themselves. When asked to explain his imagery, director Julian Schnabel remarked, "When the glaciers come out of the sea and form themselves again, you feel he is a part of everything that is there before and after."

WRAP UP

A movie's pace and rhythm are achieved through astute, time-bending editing as we've observed in this chapter. But they also can be achieved through effects, as you shall see in the next chapter.

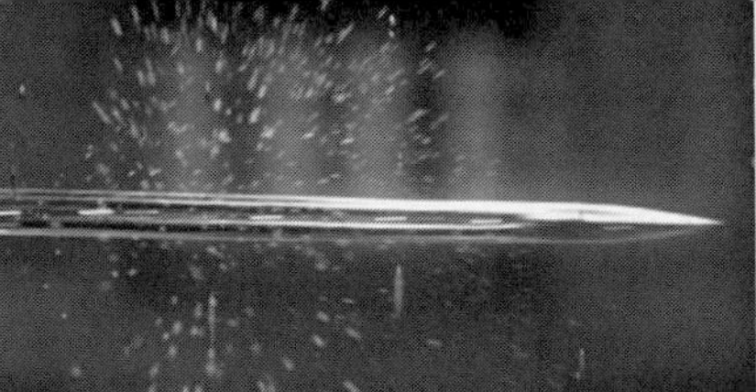

chapter 7 CUTS THAT USE TIME EFFECTS

Editing is very interesting and absorbing work because of the illusions you can create. You can span thirty years within an hour and a half. You can stretch a moment in slow motion.

– Editor Paul Hirsch, A.C.E., *Ray, Mission Impossible, Star Wars,* and many others

Just as cuts can speed up, slow down, or appear to stop the action or time, so can certain effects. In this chapter we'll identify these effects and look at how they impact the film's rhythm, pace, and story and affect the audience.

FREEZE-FRAME (A.K.A. FREEZE OR STILL FRAME)

Effect where the action holds (freezes) for as many frames as desired.

Freeze frames stop time and hold an image, idea, or plot point in the audience's mind. Habitually, they're used to prolong a character's triumph (e.g. winning a race), or tribulation (e.g. death of a loved one). Increasingly, they're used to halt the action and allow a character to directly address the audience. Ending a movie with a freeze has been popular since 1959 when director Francois Truffaut famously concluded *The 400 Blows* with a freeze of its anti-hero.

In memory
Christopher Johnson McCandless
February 12, 1968 - August 18, 1992
3

FREEZE FRAME 1: Santa knifes the cop, leaving a scar and a moment forever frozen in his memory.

Hot Fuzz

FREEZE FRAME 2: Blam! A photo flash freezes to frame a crook being thwacked.

Paprika

FREEZE FRAME 3: Freeze frames often end movies (like this one) or play under end credits.

Into the Wild

SLOW MOTION

Effect where the pace of the action is decreased from what occurred in reality in front of the camera. This retardation is accomplished during editing or, more traditionally, during filming by overcranking (running the film through the camera at a faster rate than it will be played back).

SLO MO 1: The student flips her karate master.

Kill Bill: Vol. 2

1a

The slo mo shot has many uses. Principally, it breaks down fast actions — like sports plays or car crashes — so they're easier for the audience to absorb and appreciate.

1b

1c

A slo mo typically extends a dramatic moment or shows the past.

SLO MO 2:
A good Samaritan sprints to pull Howard Hughes out of his burning plane. Will he make it in time? Slo mo prolongs the suspense.

The Aviator

SLO MO 3:
The President's motorcade moves in slo mo. Documentaries and news shows reflexively slo mo footage during editing to match the length of the narration.

Fahrenheit 911

SLO MO 4:
Explosions are regularly slo mo'd to sustain the moment.

Hot Fuzz

SLO MO 5:
Grad caps float in the air, amplifying the joy of finishing college.

Into the Wild

SLO MO 6:
A giant octopus sinks a ship in slo mo, just for the fun of it.

Pirates of the Caribbean: Dead Man's Chest

SLO MO 7:
Dance scenes are naturals for slo mo.

Mamma Mia

4

6

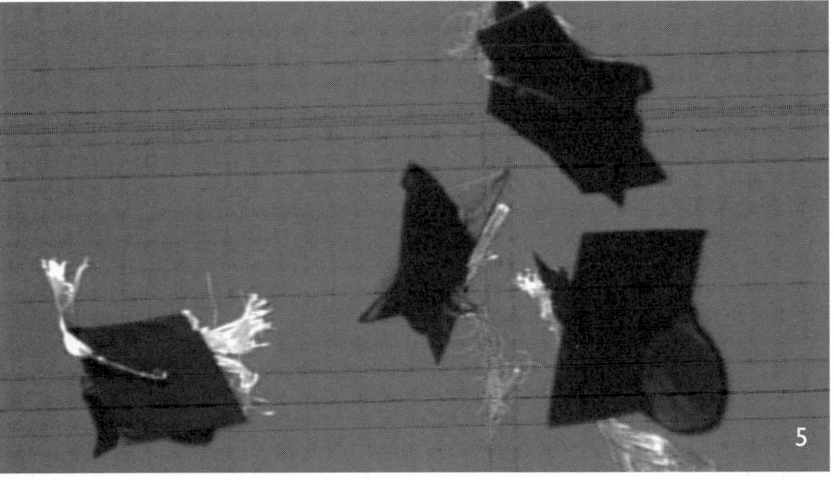
5

7

When intercut with real time or sped up shots, slo mos change the tempo of a scene, often revealing characters' thoughts and feelings. When put to music, slo mo sequences can be romantic, stretch the comedy (think of a pie catapulting across the screen), or leave the viewer gasping at the horror, tragedy, or violence of a scene.

SLO MO 8 (selected cuts): In this gut-wrenching scene, slow and regular motion shots combine with repeated, non-sequential cuts to intensify the parents' agony as they strain to protect their daughter from being shot.

Crash

4
5
6
7
8
9

SLO MO 9 (selected cuts): Slo mo shots dance with regular motion shots to slow time and accentuate the raindrops in this balletic scene. Opponent overcome, the hero sheathes his sword and the rain ceases (frame 7).

Hero

4
5
6
7

SPEED UP

Effect where the pace of the action is increased from what occurred in real time in front of the camera. This increase is accomplished during editing or, more traditionally, during filming by undercranking (running the film through the camera at a slower rate than it will be played back).

Seen far less frequently than slo mos, speed ups are commonly employed to propel a character from Point A to Point B more quickly. They're also created for comic effect, to change the tempo, or to portray the action from a character's perspective.

SPEED UP 1: As Jean-Do recovers his memory, shots rev up.

The Diving Bell and the Butterfly

SPEED UP 2: The action accelerates as Harry flies on his broomstick, a vicious, fire-breathing dragon on his tail.

Harry Potter and the Goblet of Fire

SPEED UP 3:
A worn-out Alex Supertramp stands above an L.A. freeway where traffic hyperspaces by.

Into the Wild

SPEED UP 4:
As vehicles appear and disappear at warp speed, time passes in the land of anime.

Paprika

REVERSE MOTION

Playing a shot backwards so that the filmed action takes place from end to beginning

To create a reverse, the filmed shot is reversed in the editing room, special effects house, or film lab. Occasionally, shots are filmed in reverse. For example, for safety reasons, a car is filmed as it abruptly backs away from a child. Later the shot is reversed so that the car looks like it will hit the child — as the drama required.

Reverse motion is used to explain a point or to create a comic or magical effect and can make time appear to go backwards.

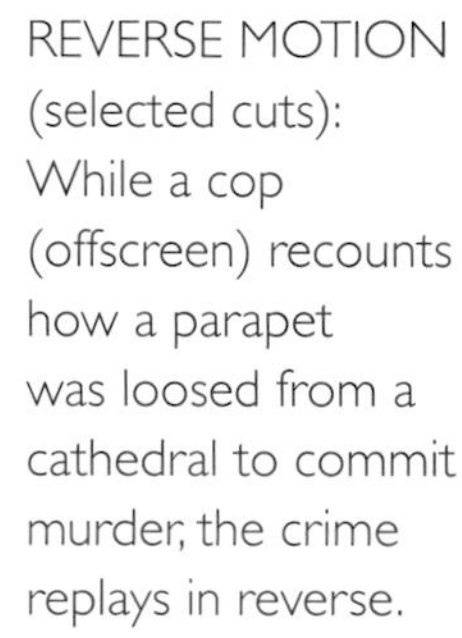

REVERSE MOTION 1 (selected cuts): While a cop (offscreen) recounts how a parapet was loosed from a cathedral to commit murder, the crime replays in reverse.

Hot Fuzz

REVERSE MOTION 2: With a stroke of headmaster Dumbledore's wand and some reverse motion, a vase appears from inside a flaming, retracting cabinet.

Harry Potter and the Goblet of Fire

2a

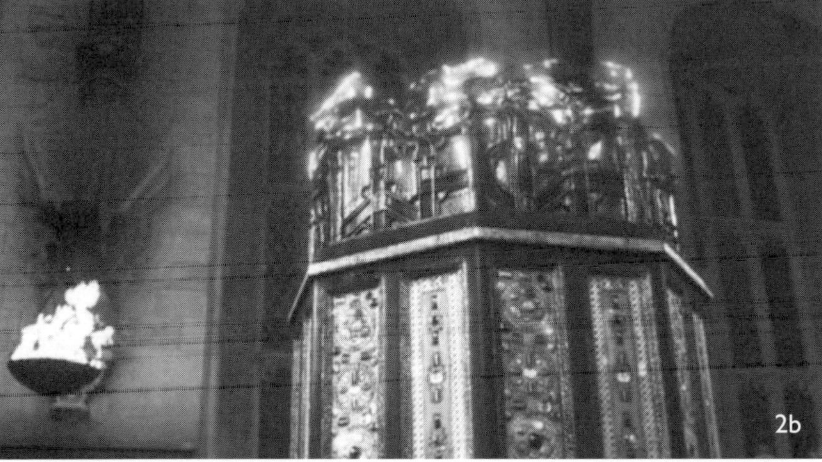

2b

2c

REVERSE MOTION 3 (selected cuts): Leading up to the climactic kiss which concludes the film, its hero relives his and his beloved's past. This recap is achieved by reverse shots: He runs backwards through a train station and she exits a bus.

Slumdog Millionaire

3a

3b

WRAP UP

Freezes, slo mos, speed ups, and reverses: In this chapter you saw how these effects can tell the story and influence the time and rhythm of cuts. In the final chapter, we'll build on this and all previous chapters to focus on the different ways in which scenes are edited.

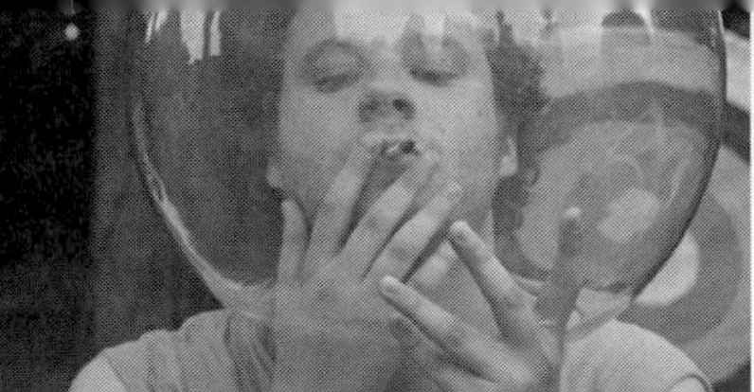

chapter 8 CUTTING SCENES

In this chapter we'll tackle the different types of edited scenes that form the building blocks of the movie. As we delve into each type, you'll discover just how efficiently and effectively they drive the story, reveal character, and communicate to the audience.

EXPOSITION

Scene at the beginning of a film that sets its time, place, situation, characters, tone, and/or theme.

A good expository scene will incorporate a dramatic hook. The hook's purpose is to deliver the movie's central conflict, mystery, or question, seducing the audience into staring at the screen for the next 90-120 minutes.

Many movies start by plunging right into the plot with a scene or two from the past, present, or future that motivates the character(s) and the rest of the movie. The first two examples demonstrate this type of exposition.

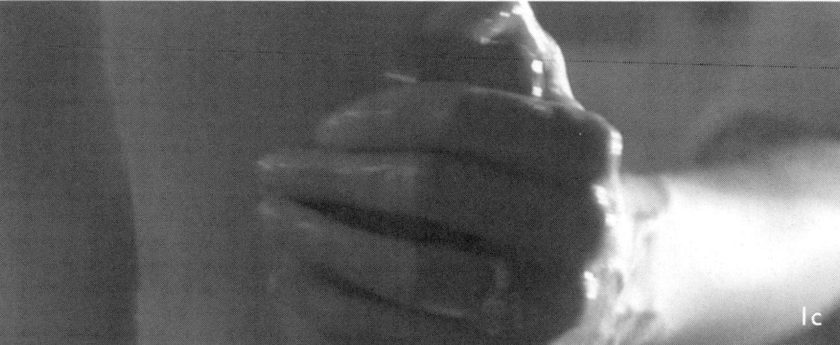

1a

EXPOSITION 1 (selected cuts): As his mother bathes him, she cajoles the young Howard Hughes to spell out the word 'quarantine.' "You are not safe," she tells him. Thus she embeds a lifelong sense of separation and phobias that clash with his outer drives and accomplishments and play out over the rest of the film.

The Aviator

EXPOSITION 2 (selected cuts): A tenacious prospector shows his grit when he blasts his mine and accidentally breaks his leg. A pair of landscape shots bookend this long opening scene; the first establishing the setting, the second showing the long trek the prospector must survive to get his leg and nugget of ore examined.

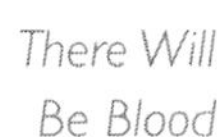

There Will Be Blood

Many other movies use establishing shots — typically wide shots or long shots — during or following the title and opening credits to create the exposition.

EXPOSITION 3 (selected cuts): Over the opening credits and accompanied by hip hop music, the main character is solidly exposed as an immature party boy who values time with his buds above all else.

Knocked Up

EXPOSITION 4 (selected cuts): Wide, ambling, Texas landscape shots, accompanied by narration, acquaint us with the film's territory and its narrator, Sheriff Ed Tom Bell. This opening scene ends by introducing us to the villain as he's taken into custody — but not for long.

No Country for Old Men

4a

4b

4c

EXPOSITION 5 (selected cuts): Nicholas Angel is swiftly established as a single-minded top cop in this opening sequence which gives his resume via voiceover and launches the comedy's snappy, off-kilter editing style.

Hot Fuzz

5a

5b

5c

5d

EXPOSITION 6 (selected cuts): With its comic book style, this title sequence re-establishes the sequel's comic book roots as it recaps what happened in the first movie and primes the audience for Spidey's latest escapade.

Spider-Man 2

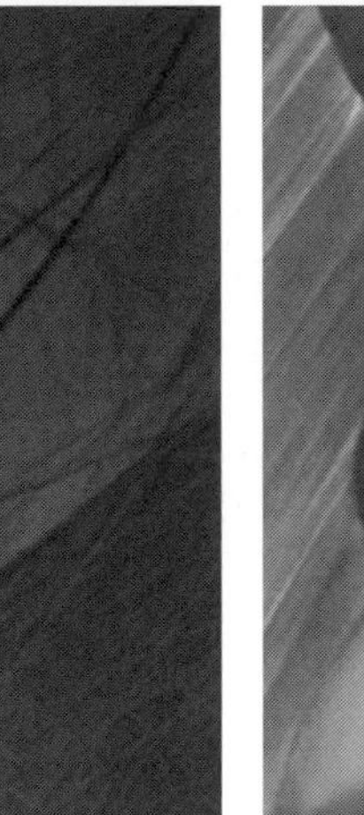

FLASHBACK

Shot, sequence of shots, or scene which transport the story into the past.

FLASHBACK 1: This movie begins as Ofelia escapes to her fantasy land, tripping the story headlong into a flashback. When the story rejoins the present near the end of the movie, we realize everything has taken place in her mind as she lies dying.

Pan's Labyrinth

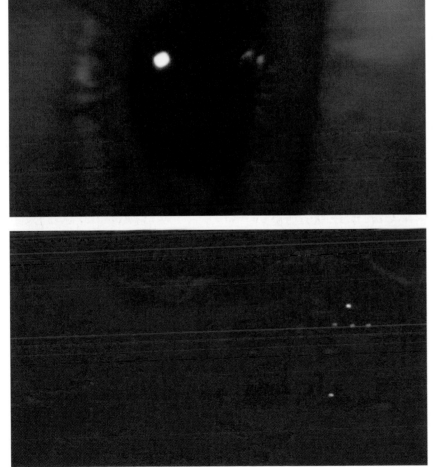

Flashbacks operate in many frequently seen ways. Commonly, they're shown in black and white or sepia and initiated by a transition effect, ordinarily a fade or a dissolve. Flashbacks can illuminate a character's feelings, thoughts, memories or earlier life (backstory) and are often used — and overused — as exposition. A flashback can also re-run an event to fix it in the viewers' minds cause them to see it anew. Flashbacks often foreshadow or tease the future, clarify plot points, or thrust the story in a new direction.

Flashbacks can be quick — consisting of flash-cuts — or long and run the length of the movie. They can also contain other flashbacks and occur in non-chronological order.

No matter how a flashback operates, it is vital that while it is sending the story backwards in time, it drive the film forward.

A flashback can mire a character in the past, help them through difficult situations or strong emotions such as grief or anger, or spur them to make a decision or act.

FLASHBACK 2: Buried alive in a coffin, The Bride recalls her karate training thanks to a flashback, and starts to break free.

Kill Bill: Vol. 2

FLASHBACK 3: Bourne flashes back to his tortuous programming to be a CIA assassin and resolves to stay on the run from the agency.

The Bourne Ultimatum

FLASHBACK 4 (selected cuts): After his wife's assassination, widower Justin Quayle grieves.

The Constant Gardener

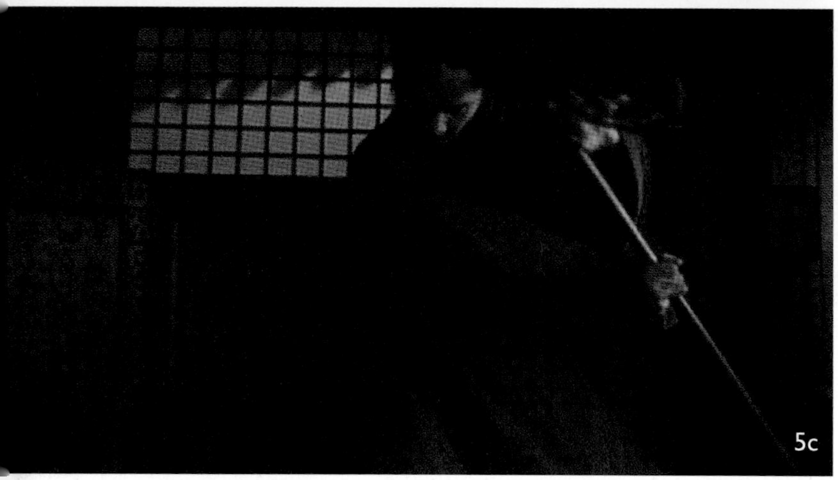

Storm! Storm! Storm! 5a

5c

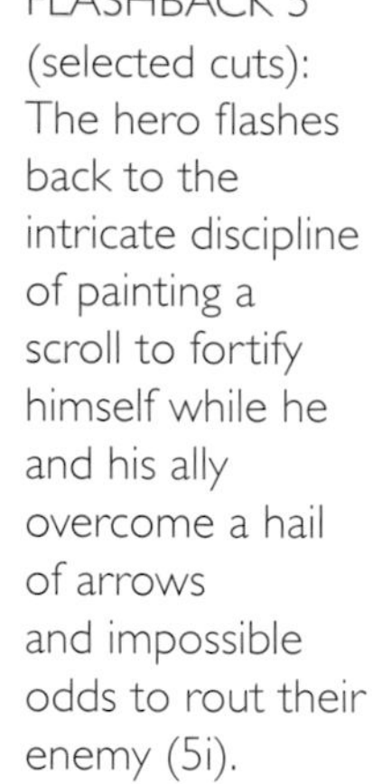

FLASHBACK 5 (selected cuts): The hero flashes back to the intricate discipline of painting a scroll to fortify himself while he and his ally overcome a hail of arrows and impossible odds to rout their enemy (5i).

Hero

5f

5g

5h

5i

5j

FLASHFORWARD

Shot, sequence of shots, or scene which transports the story into the future.

Flashforwards work in a variety of ways to keep the audience engrossed and the story rolling along. They can presage upcoming events or disclose parts of the story that have not yet been told but may be dramatized later in greater detail. Frequently, a flashforward bares a character's hopes and fears for the future in the form of a dream or nightmare. Like flashbacks, flashforwards may start a movie or be inserted along the way.

FLASHFORWARD 1: After Lightening McQueen has a nightmare where he's being chased on the racetrack by a reaper, he decides to skedaddle out of town.

Cars

FLASHFORWARD 2: This film's first scene is a flashforward centered on a detective exploring a crime scene at night. The second scene is a flashback to the previous morning. The story then develops chronologically, returning to the initial flashforward scene near the end.

Crash

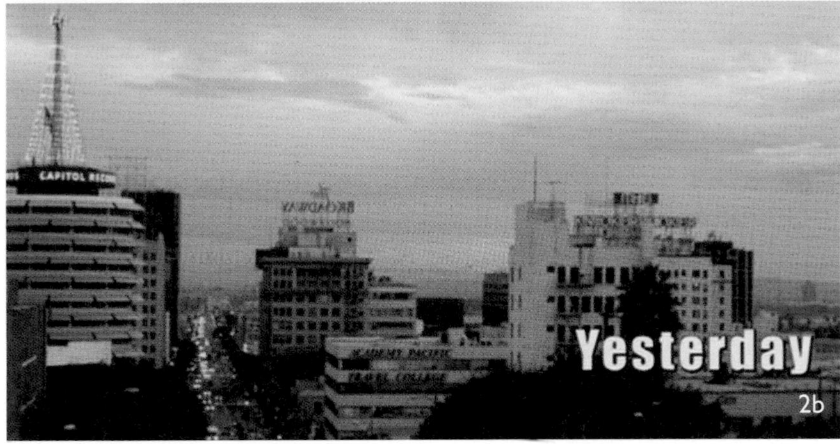

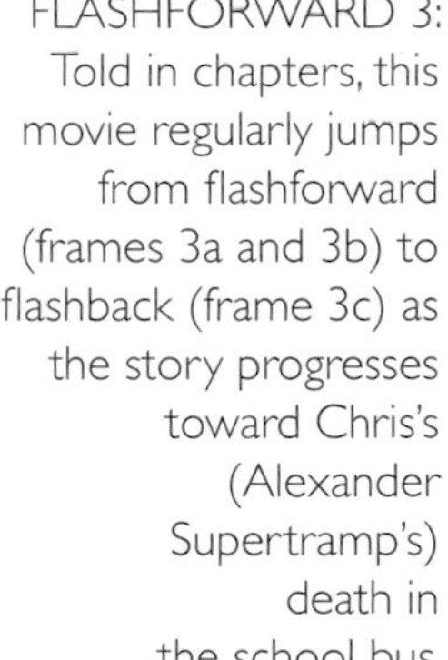

FLASHFORWARD 3: Told in chapters, this movie regularly jumps from flashforward (frames 3a and 3b) to flashback (frame 3c) as the story progresses toward Chris's (Alexander Supertramp's) death in the school bus.

Into the Wild

Emory University, Atlanta, Ga.
Two years before "Magic" bus...
3c

FLASHFORWARDS 4-7:
A jigsaw puzzle of flashforwards and flashbacks, this biopic depicts singer Edith Piaf's life.

La Vie en Rose

4
The film begins with a flashforward to her collapse at a concert in Manhattan in 1959.

5
1918: A lipsticked young Edith is raised in a whorehouse. Flashforward to: 1935: An adult Edith prepares to sing.

6
1918: Her surrogate mother wails when Edith is taken away from the whorehouse. Flashforward to: 1959: After a triumphant tour, Edith arrives in Paris.

7
1935: An exuberant Edith on New Year's Eve. Flashforward to: 1963: An arthritic Edith, battered by poor health.

MONTAGE

Derived from the French word "to mount," a succinct, self-contained sequence of images inserted to convey or summarize facts, feelings, or thoughts.

MONTAGE 1 (selected cuts): Natural life with natural sounds and no music or narration document Baghdad in the run-up to war.

Fahrenheit 911

Usually a montage functions like a musical interlude, bridging time, place, or knowledge with its evolving collage of images. Music and narration habitually replace dialogue in montage scenes. However, some montages contain deliberate, recurring sounds or natural sounds recorded at the scene. A few are silent.

Montages have many themes — dramatic, comic, news — to list the major categories. A few montage themes have reached cliché status and become spoof material such as the "Getting over the loss of a love" montage, the "Getting fit" montage, and the "Preparing for the big event or showdown" montage.

To compose a montage, shots can be pulled from many sources: dailies, newsreel footage, YouTube, TV shows, etc. When cut together, these shots make a scene that is much bigger than the sum of its cuts.

MONTAGE 2 (selected cuts): A series of dissolves along with voiceover and music guide a trip down memory lane to the glory days of Radiator Springs' and back to its faded present.

Cars

MONTAGE 3 (selected cuts): Postcard-like text and music transport the audience to Alaska in this expository montage near the beginning of the movie.

Into the Wild

4a

4b

MONTAGE 4 (selected cuts): Oysters complemented by voiceover and music feed this fantasy seduction.

The Diving Bell and the Butterfly

It feels like we met yesterday.
4c

4d

4e

PARALLEL ACTION

Editing two (or more) independent lines of action together so that the characters, settings, or subjects do not interact directly and are unaware of each other.

PARALLEL ACTION 1: The often parallel lives of black and white Los Angelenos are seen in parallel action until a carjacking causes the two worlds to collide.

Crash

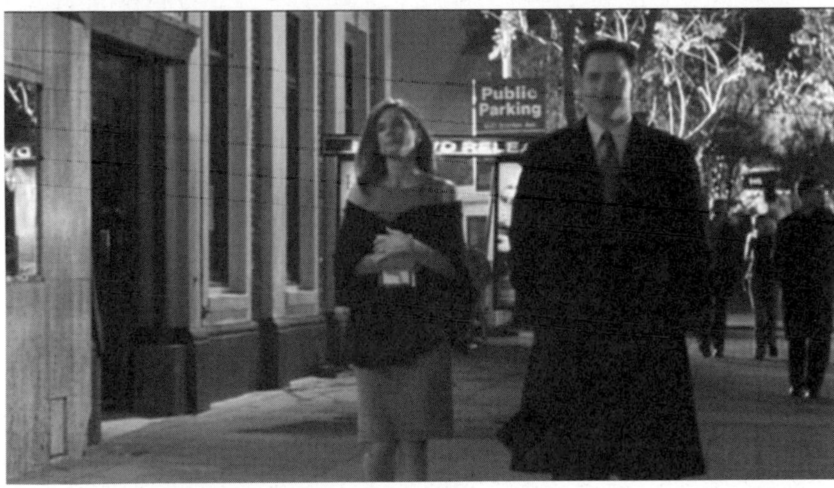

Parallel action regularly kicks off films, introducing strangers going about their separate lives and making the audience wonder what they have in common or impatient to see them meet. Often, the audience is ahead of the characters in a parallel action scene: It knows the two people are going to intersect and that it's just a question of when, why, and how.

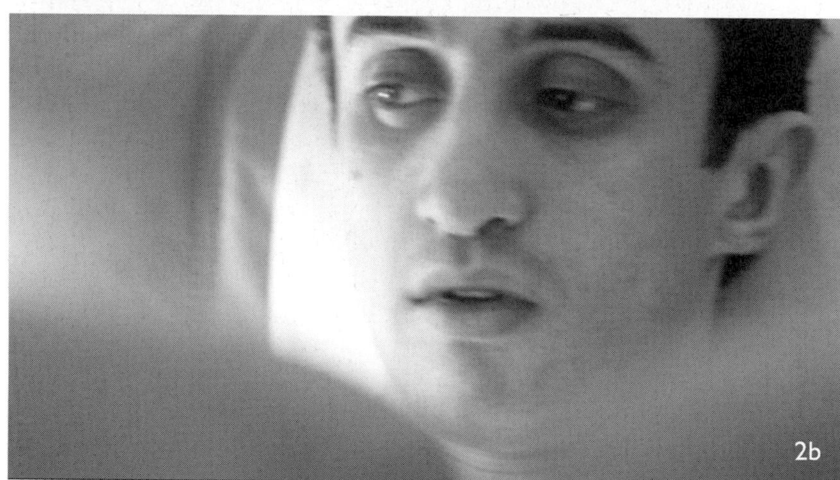

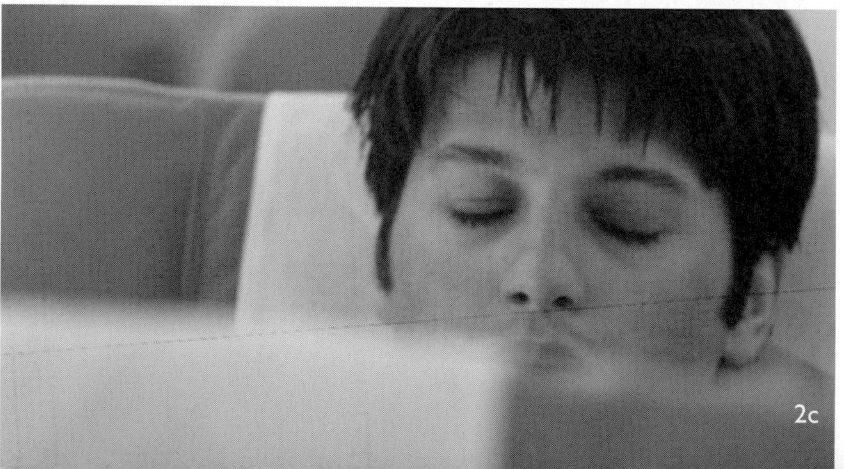

PARALLEL ACTION 2 (selected cuts): Passengers go about their mundane business while the hijackers prepare to carry out their deadly mission.

United 93

2d
2e
2f
2g

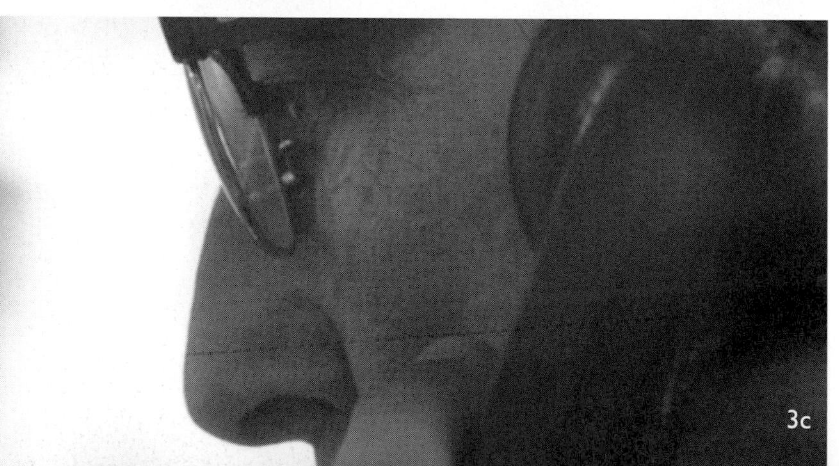

PARALLEL ACTION 3 (selected cuts): When their target's innocent daughter returns home unexpectedly and picks up the phone, the team of Israeli counter-terrorists frantically scurries to alert each other and diffuse a bomb (last frame) to abort an assassination.

Munich

3d
3e
3f
3g
3h
3i

CROSS CUTTING

Editing two (or more) dependent lines of action together so that the characters, settings, or subjects interact directly and are aware of each other.

In cross cut scenes, the characters are linked — and may be furiously interacting, e.g. the cops closing in on the robbers or the firefighters racing toward the people trapped in the burning building. Often part of a film's climax, crosscutting brings characters and situations together, usually tightening the dramatic pace and ratcheting up the conflict.

1a

1b

1c

1d

CROSS CUTTING 1 (selected cuts): Four scenes are intercut (cross cut) as the movie climaxes:

1a) Sylvia Llewelyn Davies lies dying as her friend J. M. Barrie dashes between her death bed and

1b) the premiere of his play, Peter Pan.

1c) Her son Peter, watches the play he inspired.

1d) J. M. Barrie ends his marriage.

Finding Neverland

CROSS CUTTING 2 (selected cuts): Bourne warily strides to hook up with a nervous reporter as the CIA is hot on their trail, in this tense action scene created by cross cuts.

The Bourne Ultimatum

OVERLAPPING ACTION

A variation of cross cutting where a series of shots with repeating actions, often from different angles or points of view, are intercut within a scene (or scenes).

OVERLAPPING ACTION 1: Repeated head turns of the main character (frames 1-2) and the crowd (frames 4-7) heighten the fright of seeing the alien advance (frame 3).

War of the Worlds

Overlapping action exaggerates the action for dramatic or comic impact and stretches time.

4
5
6
7

and the archers are peerless
in their range and accuracy.

and the archers are peerless
in their range and accuracy.

OVERLAPPING ACTION 2: The archers' repetitive bow lifting actions draw out the wait for the battle to begin.

Hero

OVERLAPPING ACTION 3: Repeated slo mo shots of the cops firing, intercut with the regular motion shots of the bar, intensify and extend this shoot out sequence.

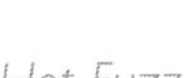

Hot Fuzz

FINAL WRAP UP

We began by looking at basic cuts and moved on to match cuts, jump cuts, flash cuts, smash cuts, cross cuts, and parallel action. We covered a variety of effects including fades, wipes, greenscreens and mattes and discovered some witty and extraordinary edits along the way. Across 35 movies and all film genres, these cuts took us to ancient China, modern-day Alaska, a cartoon Paris, the magical realm of Harry Potter and countless other places — into the hearts and minds of a bevy of fictional and historical characters.

I sincerely hope you have enjoyed looking at these highly illustrative film frames as much as I have. And I hope that next time the theatre lights go down and a movie's cuts begin to tell the story, you will have a deeper view and awe of what's projected on the screen.

If you are making your own films, my wish is that you use what you've absorbed here to better your creations.

Film editing mimics the way we see, think, dream, feel, and sense. The audience tenses and holds its breath with tight pacing, and breathes out and cheers when the pacing relaxes and the plot achieves a waited for climax. Movies not only affect our breathing but they get under our skin and into our hearts and psyches. Increasingly, they cross into our dreams, nightmares, and life experience; we discuss the stories we see with others and they converge, unintentionally, with our own life tales. The convergence becomes the stories told and retold 'round the campfire — the café, the bar, the family room, the car.

Each generation has its unique truths and fables. Go discover yours. Tell your tales. Make your movies. And make them well, so others will listen and fold them into their lives and retell them long after you made your last edit. We all look forward to seeing them.

SYNOPSIS OF FILMS

The Aviator

Directed by Martin Scorsese, this biopic recounts the life of billionaire Howard Hughes (Leonardo DiCaprio) from boyhood until his early 40s in the 1940s. Hughes flies, designs, and manufactures new planes and founds Hughes Aircraft with the help of his right hand man, Noah Dietrich (John C. Reilly). He also directs and produces movies and has liaisons with actresses: Katherine Hepburn (Cate Blanchett), Jean Harlow (Gwen Stefani), and Ava Gardner (Kate Beckinsale). Along the way he butts heads with Pan American airlines president Juan Tripp (Alec Baldwin) and Senator Ralph Owen Brewster (Alan Alda) as well as the Hollywood establishment. He also suffers several prolonged mental breakdowns during which he isolates himself from everyone.

Babel

This complex movie consists of stories about characters in four different cultures: Morocco, Japan, Mexico, and United States. Two brothers in remote, mountainous Morocco become bored while tending goats. One taunts the other into shooting at a tourist bus on the distant highway. An American couple — disconnected due to the death of their baby — is on the bus. The wife (Cate Blanchett) is hit and her husband (Brad Pitt) frantically seeks help in the nearest town.

Meanwhile, at their home in San Diego, the Americans' faithful nanny (Adriana Barraza) tends to their two children. Forbidden to secure alternative childcare and desperate to attend her son's wedding in Mexico, she takes the kids across the border. All enjoy the wedding but the car ride back north with her ne'er-do-well nephew (Gael Garcia Bernal) strands them in the desert with tragic consequences.

Across the world in Tokyo, a severely hearing-impaired teenager (Rinko Kikuchi) deals with her mother's death and her need for love. Her father, a successful businessman enmeshed in his own sorrow, isolates himself in work and ignores her.

The four cultures and stories converge: The Moroccan boy/shooter is found, his gun is traced to the Japanese businessman, the American couple survives the shooting and takes action about their children's disappearance.

The Bourne Ultimatum

In this third film of the thriller trilogy derived from Robert Ludlum's books, renegade CIA agent Jason Bourne (Matt Damon) is still deciphering his own identity while on the run from the CIA establishment, specifically Section Chief Noah Vosen (David Strathairn) and Deputy Director Pamela Landy (Joan Allen). Their department oversees Blackbriar, a secret rendition program that nabs suspected terrorists and turns them over to nations that don't balk at torture. Bourne finds out about the program and arranges to learn more from a reporter, (Paddy Considine). The CIA is hot on their trail. They gun down the reporter but Bourne eludes them.

The chase to capture or kill Bourne goes international, moving from Moscow to London to Turin to Madrid to Tangiers. It ends with Bourne apparently shot and drowned in New York City's East River. However, he pops above water in the last frame of the movie, priming the audience for another Bourne movie.

Brokeback Mountain

Two Montana cowboys find the love of their life in each other and face the test of time, family upbringings, wives and children, starting in the 1960s. The late Heath Ledger starred as Ennis del Mar, Jake Gyllenhaal played Jack Twist, and Ang Lee won the Academy Award for best directing in this drama based on the Annie Proux short story.

Cars

Characters are cars in this animated movie. Main caracter, er, character Lightening McQueen (voiced by Owen Wilson), a hot shot rookie race car, determines to win the big Piston Cup Championship race. On the way to doing this, he is sidetracked to Radiator Springs, a town on Route 66 that time has left behind. Forced to stay there to pay off a debt, he gets to know the town's characters, including a 1951 Hudson (voiced by Paul Newman) and grows up a bit. The town characters then help him win the big race.

The Constant Gardener

Adapted from the novel by John le Carré, this story takes place mainly in Kenya where an introverted British diplomat Justin Quayle (Ralph Fiennes), grieves for his dead, politically active wife Tessa (Rachel Weisz). He soon realizes that her death wasn't accidental and determines to discover why she was killed. His investigation leads to corruption between pharmaceutical corporations and government bureaucracies and ultimately, his own murder.

Corpse Bride

Tim Burton contrived this gothic animated tale set in Great Britain during the Victorian age. Victor Van Dort (voiced by Johnny Depp) fumbles his vows and his chance to wed his betrothed (voiced by Emily Watson). Wandering in the forest at night to practice his vows for a re-match, he unwittingly marries a corpse bride (voiced by Helena Bonham Carter). She's overjoyed to live happily ever after with him in her land of the dead. He spends the rest of the movie negotiating between his betrothed and his bride and rectifying the situation.

Crash

Winner of the Academy award for best picture in 2005, this drama focuses on LA's intersecting cultures — black, white, Hispanic, Asian, and Middle Eastern — as they crash into each other in a series of interwoven plots.

The Da Vinci Code

Based on the bestselling book, this biblical thriller begins with the murder of a curator in the Paris's Louvre museum. The murdered curator is the grandfather of a police cryptographer (Audrey Tatou). Interpol is certain that visiting Professor of Symbology (Tom Hanks) is the killer. Needing his expertise and knowing he's innocent, she springs him from Interpol. On the lam, the pair pursues the clues. They lead to biblical times and the bloodline of Jesus Christ as well as to a religious sect hell bent on suppressing this knowledge.

The Diving Bell and the Butterfly

Editor of the French fashion magazine Elle, Jean-Dominic "Jean-Do" Bauby (Mathieu Amaric) is living the high life until he has a stroke at age 43 in 1995. It leaves him paralyzed, except for his left eye. The film begins as he comes to consciousness, reborn as an invalid with his mental faculties intact but unable to communicate. The audience hears his thoughts via voice over narration and spends the movie watching him cope with his misfortune.

At first, Jean-Do wants to die and feels trapped, like a diver in an old-fashioned diving bell. He escapes to memories, dreams, and fantasies to free himself, as he imagines, like a butterfly emerging from a chrysalis. He remembers having a close conversation while shaving his 92 year old father (Max von Sydow). He flashes back to his childhood and fantasizes romances — making love on the beach and having a seductive oyster lunch. His children visit him on Father's day. He fears their rejection but they accept him in his new condition. A speech therapist (Marie-Josée Croze), works out a method for him to use his eye to blink and spell out words. He then painstakingly dictates a book about his life to his publisher's assistant (Anne Consigny). *The Diving Bell and the Butterfly* becomes a best seller after his death.

Fahrenheit 911

In this documentary, director Michael Moore turns a critical lens on how President George W. Bush acted on September 11, 2001 and afterwards and on how his administration's actions affected U.S. soldiers, their families and other Americans as well as Iraqi citizens.

Finding Neverland

A fictionalized tale of how a widow (Kate Winslet) and her four boys inspired J. M. Barrie (Johnny Depp) to write *Peter Pan*.

Harry Potter and the Goblet of Fire

The fourth movie based on the series of Harry Potter books begins with Harry (Daniel Radcliffe) and best friends Ron (Rupert Grint) and Hermione (Emma Watson) attending the Quidditch World Cup Final. After the match, a melee erupts, instigated by the menacing followers of the villain Lord Voldemort (Ralph Fiennes) and the trio manages to escape.

Soon the three wizards-in-training are on the train to Hogwarts School where they meet a new, monoculared teacher: Mad Eye Moody (Brendan Gleeson). Harry is chosen to compete in the Triwizard tournament when his name mysteriously emerges from the goblet of fire. Along with bad press from journalist Rita Skeeter (Miranda Richardson) and estrangement from Ron and Hermione, he faces a series of tournament challenges, including a face off with a fire breathing dragon. These climax in a duel with Lord Voldemort and schoolmate Neville's tragic death.

Hero

Quentin Tarantino lent his name as presenter of this epic samurai film set in ancient China and directed by Zhang Yimou, the prodigious Chinese director. It tells the tale of a fictional hero called Nameless (Jet Li), who protects the emperor by fighting off assassins and attacking armies. The film contains stunning cinematography, especially evident in the exquisitely balletic sword fight scenes of male on male, male on female, and female on female combat.

Hot Fuzz

At the start of this fast paced British comedy, London top cop Nicholas Angel (Simon Pegg) expects a promotion. Instead, his jealous boss (Bill Nighy) assigns him to a small, trouble free hamlet. Partnered with the police chief's son (Nick Frost), Angel discovers the town has trouble — with a capital M for many murders.

Into the Wild

Sean Penn directed this biopic, based on Jon Krakauer's haunting book of the same title. The film goes back and forth in time and events as it recounts the life of 24 year old Chris McCandless (Emile Hirsch). Renaming himself Alex Supertramp, he adventures across the U.S. by thumb, kayak, and on foot for two years after college graduation. In 1992 he sets off on a solo trip into the wilds of Alaska. Turning an abandoned school bus into his home, he keeps a diary of his odyssey, which ends with his death by starvation.

Kill Bill Vol. 2

The Bride (Uma Thurman), a martial arts expert and former paid assassin, completes her quest for revenge in this Quentin Tarantino directed film. First, she escapes from being buried alive in a coffin by Budd (Michael Madsen) and sets out across the desert on her mission.

Thinking he's killed The Bride, Budd goes to the desert trailer of eye-patched Elle Driver (Daryl Hannah) for a monetary reward. She kills him by planting a deadly snake in the suitcase of pay off money. Then she's surprised by The Bride who emerges from the desert and attacks her, flying feet first though the wall of her trailer. After a fierce fight, Elle is eliminated. The Bride then tracks down her final target — ex-boss and ex-lover Bill (David Carradine) — who is taking care of their daughter. She kills him before he can kill her and sets off with her daughter for a new life.

Knocked Up
After a boozy one night stand, successful Alison Scott (Katherine Heigl) becomes pregnant by slacker Ben Stone (Seth Rogen). These two ill-suited, twenty-somethings spend the rest of this dramedy growing up. The movie concludes with their committing to each other and living together with their baby girl.

La Vie en Rose
The harrowing life of French singer Edith Piaf (Marion Cotillard) unfolds in flashbacks and flashforwards from her birth in 1915 to her death in 1963.

Lust, Caution
Adapting an Eileen Change story, director Ang Lee tells the story of a plot to assassinate Mr. Yee (Tony Leung) a Japanese collaborator during WWII. Wong Chia (Tang Wei) is assigned to gain his trust by befriending his wife (Joan Chen) whom she joins for mahjong, and seducing him. Their rough tumble affair takes on a life of its own: As love, hate, and murderous intentions grow, it becomes clear that only one of them will get out of it alive.

Mamma Mia
Desiring to meet her father, a bride-to-be (Amanda Seyfried) invites three potential candidates (Colin Firth, Stellan Skarsgard, and Pierce Brosnan) to her wedding without telling her mother (Meryl Streep). This adaptation of the Broadway musical builds a plot from the songs of 1970s pop group Abba and sets it on a paradisiacal Greek island.

Man on Wire
This Academy Award winning documentary recalls the balletic feat of Phillipe Petit, tightrope walker extraordinaire, and his rag tag band of friends and co-conspirators: After two years of choreographing the rigging and the illegal trespass, they placed him on a wire between the twin towers of NY's World Trade Center in 1974 where he sky (scraper) walked for 45 minutes.

Munich
Steven Spielberg directed and produced this dark and thought-provoking historical drama about the moral aspects of international terrorism. The story begins with the slaughter of the eleven Israeli athletes during the 1972 Olympics in Munich by Black September, a Palestinian terrorist group. Avner (Eric Bana) is recruited to lead a four-man Israeli squad to kill those responsible. Through trial and error, the squad succeeds, but Avner, the film's conscience, has moral doubts from the start. He quits the squad and Israel to take up permanent residence in Brooklyn, NY.

In the film's final scene, set in New York City around 1975, his recruiter (Jeffrey Rush) refuses his invitation to break bread with Avner and his family. The two men part and the camera pans to show Manhattan, including the twin towers — a last call out to the destructiveness of terrorism.

No Country for Old Men
It's 1980 and the rules of law have changed, Sheriff Ed Tom Bell (Tommy Lee Jones) tells us over a series of shots of Texas's open plains as the movie starts. This sequence ends with the entrance of the proof of his words: villain Anton Chigurh (Javier Bardem). He's out to retrieve two million dollars of drug money. The drama continues as Bell looks for Chigurh and Chigurh kills anyone who blocks his path to the money.

Pan's Labyrinth
In the mountains of northern Spain it's 1944 and rebels are still holding out against fascist dictator Franco. Ten year old Ofelia (Ivana Baquero) arrives with her fragile, pregnant mother, (Ariadna Gil) at the military outpost commanded by her brutal stepfather (Sergi López). To deal with her lonely situation, Ofelia enters an underground fantasy world. As her stepfather hunts down, tortures, and kills rebels and her mother's pregnancy becomes life-threatening, Vidal's housekeeper Mercedes (Maribel Verdú), takes Ofelia under her wing. In the end, her fantasy world helps Ofelia cope with her mother's death in childbirth and her own death at the hands of her stepfather.

Paprika

Adapted from a sci fi story, this innovative Japanese anime movie, crosses the borders between reality, dreams, and cinema. Set in the near future, the plot revolves around a dream recording device that falls into the wrong hands before research scientists have fully tested it. Eighteen year old Paprika is the dream detective and alter ego of one of the researchers. She and a police detective, who secretly wishes to be a film director, are brought into help recover the device.

Pirates of the Caribbean, Dead Man's Chest

In this second movie based on the Disneyland theme ride, pirate Jack Sparrow (Johnny Depp) returns and draws reluctant friends Will Turner (Orlando Bloom) and Elizabeth Swan (Keira Knightley) into his misadventures. They deal with an assortment of buccaneer woes: sea monsters, unruly islanders, a conniving seer (Tia Dalma), and a demanding Davy Jones (Bill Nighy).

Ratatouille

The animated story of a country rat with the soul of a gourmet who, with the help of a human sous chef and the tutelage of a TV chef, winds up the top chef in Paris in charge of his own bistro.

Rope

Two college men living together in an apartment in Manhattan decide to test philosopher Friedrich Nietzsche's theory of superior men. They strangle a prep school chum and deposit his body in a prominent chest in their living room right before his fiancée, family, and their philosophy professor show up for cocktails. The rest of the evening is a cat and mouse game as the professor zeroes in on their crime and misapplied philosophy.

Slumdog Millionaire

An 18 year old assistant chai-wallah (tea server) (Dev Patel) relives his harsh, impoverished life growing up in Mumbai as he is questioned and tortured by the police who suspect him of cheating on a TV game show. He proves his innocence, wins a million dollars, and is reunited with his childhood sweetheart (Freida Pinto).

Spider-Man 2

This time out, Spider-Man (Tobey Maguire), confronts a new adversary — mad scientist Doc Ock (Alfred Molina) whose octopus arms form a formidable weapon. Spidey also must fight to keep his girlfriend Mary Jane Watson (Kirsten Dunst), who becomes engaged to another man. All this plus school, work, and the weighty responsibility of being Spider-Man sends him on various adventures in and around Manhattan.

There Will Be Blood

A ruthless miner (Daniel-Day Lewis) becomes a rich oil man through manipulation and murder in turn-of-the-century California.

Underworld Evolution

This second Underworld movie, centers on vampire Selene (Kate Beckinsale) as vampires and werewolves battle above and below ground to put ancient massacres and alliances to rest.

United 93

A well-researched, yet speculative account of what took place on the ground and aboard the plane where passengers thwarted the hijackers' plans, forcing it to crash into the Pennsylvania countryside on September 11, 2001.

War of the Worlds

The weekend doesn't start off well for New Jersey dock worker and divorced dad Ray Ferrier (Tom Cruise); Rachel, his young daughter (Dakota Fanning) and Robbie, his teenage son (Justin Chatwin) are making a rare visit. It gets worse: Aliens strike — three legged blood sucking, laser-firing, vaporizing creatures from another planet.

Ray commandeers a van and drives them toward Boston where the children's mother is staying. Forced by a desperate crowd to abandon the van, they board a ferry, only to be pitched into the dark waters of the Hudson River when the aliens capsize it. Robbie takes off with the Army and Ray and Rachel take refuge in the basement of Harlan Ogilvy (Tim Robbins) who has lost his mind after seeing his family and others destroyed. The aliens send probes around corners, terrorizing the three of them. Ray manages to escape with Rachel, only to fight off an alien with hand grenades.

Finally the aliens die from an earthly virus to which they have no immunity. Ray and Rachel make it to Boston where Robbie shows up. The three of them have created a lasting bond and Ray has gained respect from his ex-wife. The remake is an updated version of the science fiction book by H. G. Wells and was directed by Steven Spielberg.

GLOSSARY

A.C.E. American Cinema Editors. An honorary society of editors committed to the craft of editing. A.C.E. always follows a member's name on screen.

action match. Matching the action (movement or motion) of characters or objects in one shot to the action in the next shot where the action continues or completes.

AMPAS. Academy of Motion Picture Arts and Sciences. The "Academy" hands out the annual Oscar awards, holds screenings throughout the year to honor US filmmakers, and promotes the recognition and preservation of motion pictures.

blue screen. Same as greenscreen except that a blue screen is used. See greenscreen.

black out. When a shot cuts to black.

close-up (CU). A shot framed close, usually on the face and neck of a person.

continuity. Maintaining the physical relationships, performance, action, and narrative flow of the filmed scene from cut to cut (or, during filming, from shot to shot).

coverage. Angles filmed in addition to the master shot: close-ups, medium shots, over-the-shoulder shots, etc.

cross cutting. Editing two (or more) dependent lines of action together — characters, settings, or subjects — that interact directly and are aware of each other.

crossing the line. Ignoring the invisible line in every camera set up that bisects the scene horizontally at 180.° Crossing the line results in two angles that when cut together appear to make people or objects jump out of position.

cut. The joining together of two different shots, or occasionally, two parts of the same shot.

cutter. Film term for editor. See editor.

cutaway. Any shot that will be used to cut away from the action in the master shot. Term used interchangeably with insert. Technically, a cutaway is filmed during the production phase.

cutpoint. Place in a shot where editor decides to cut to another shot.

dailies. Footage that arrives daily in the editing room from the previous day's shoot. Dailies used to arrive on film but since most films are edited on digital systems these days, dailies now invariably arrive on DV (digital video) cassettes.

development. Phase of a project where the director, producers, casting director, principal talent (actors) are hired and the script is set. Development follows greenlighting and precedes the preproduction phase.

digital editing system. Computer editor uses to cut digital audio and video. Referred to by many names including: digital system, editor, and brand name, e.g. the Avid, etc.

dissolve. A transitional effect where the first/outgoing shot disappears as the second/incoming shot appears.

editor. Person responsible for putting all the footage together to create the finished piece: movie, video, commercial, etc.

extreme close-up (ECU). A shot framed so tight that if it's on a person's face you just see the eyes.

exposition sequence. Series of shots or scenes at the beginning of a film that set its time, place, situation, characters, tone, and/or theme.

eyeline. A character's line of vision — the direction in which their eyes are looking.

fade in. A dissolve to a filmed shot from black, sometimes white, and once in awhile yellow, blue, or another color.

fade out. A dissolve from a filmed shot to black, sometimes white, and once in awhile yellow, blue, or another color.

film lab. Facility that produces the final film reels that are projected in the theatres. The lab also creates the final special effects on film. Labs used to hum with the bustle of producing film dailies and the final prints for movie theatres. But the digital age and its need for dailies on digital tape, not film, and — coming soon — digital projection has put this era in the past. Many film labs have partnered with post production facilities to stay alive.

flashback. Shot, sequence of shots, or scene which transports the story into the past.

flashforward. Shot, sequence of shots, or scene which transports the story into the future.

flash frame. A frame of black or white inserted between two cuts.

freeze frame, a.k.a. freeze or still frame. Effect where the action holds (freezes) for as many frames as desired.

full shot (FS). A shot framed to include the whole person or object being filmed.

greenlight. To formally approve a project and acquire its financing. Once it's greenlit (greenlighted), a project moves into the development phase.

greenscreen. Creating a new shot by compositing (merging) two shots together. Shot 1, a live action shot, is the background. Shot 2, the greenscreen shot, contains the subject (talent) and is the foreground. When the two shots are composited, the greenscreen washes out and the subject appears to react to what's happening in the background, e.g. a farmer reacting to a giant spider.

insert. Any shot that will be used to cut away from the action in the master shot. Term used interchangeably with cutaway. Technically, an insert is filmed during the postproduction phase.

inset. Effect where a reduced shot is placed on another shot, typically to highlight a detail of the main shot.

intercut. Taking two sequential scenes and cutting between them so that the scenes advance and complete together. Intercut scenes are either parallel action or cross cut scenes.

invisible editing. Editing that is so smooth that viewers become engrossed in the movie and don't notice the individual cuts.

jump cut. A cut where objects or characters appear to jump because the shots are too similar. Technically, this is due to the camera angles of the two shots being less than 30° apart.

long shot (LS). A shot framed long that focuses on the action from a distance.

master shot. Shot that encompasses all the action in a scene from beginning to end. Although a master routinely starts framed close on a small object and can zoom and pan as needed to capture the action, it mostly stays wide to frame all the action.

match cut. A continuity cut where the majority of the elements are duplicated (matched) from the first shot to the second shot. The elements to match are: screen direction, eyeline, camera angle and framing, props, sound (wording, volume, or pacing), weather, wardrobe, hair, make-up, lighting, color, and action.

matte shot. Cutting a hole in a shot and placing (matting or keying) another shot in that hole.

medium close-up (MCU). Between a CU and an MS, a MCU is filmed from the shoulders up through the top of the person's head.

medium shot (MS). A shot framed from the waist or chest up through the top of the person's head.

mismatch. A cut in which continuity is lost due to a difference between elements such as action, eyeline, camera framing, camera position, prop, wardrobe, or makeup. See match cut.

montage. A succinct, self-contained sequence of images inserted to convey facts, feelings, or thoughts that usually functions as a transition in time or place.

morph. A special effect where one object or image transforms into another, e.g. a man turns into a monster.

Moviola. Upright film editing machine all but displaced by digital editing systems today.

MPAA. Motion Picture Academy of Arts. The board that rates feature films, bestowing a G, PG, PG-13, R, NC-17, or X rating and protects them against piracy.

over the shoulder (O/S or OTS). A shot from the waist or chest up that includes the shoulder of one character while focusing on the other character.

overhead (OH). Often filmed from a crane, an overhead shot looks down on the scene from above.

overlap. A cut where picture and sound cut in at different times so that one overlaps (extends beyond) the other.

pan. Shot where camera moves horizontally left to right or vice versa.

parallel action. Editing two (or more) independent lines of action together — characters, settings, or subjects — that do not interact directly and are unaware of each other.

point-of-view shot (POV). A variation of a reverse shot, a POV shot corresponds exactly to where a character is looking; it is what they're seeing.

postproduction. The final creation phase of a show during which all editing and finishing work take place. Also referred to as editing, editorial, or post. Postproduction is followed by the distribution and exhibition phases of the movie.

postproduction house. Facility where the final cut of a show is reproduced in the digital format contractually required for airing on television or screening in theatres. Post houses also produce digital dailies and perform a myriad of other post production tasks. Frequently, they rent cutting rooms and screening rooms and provide free meals in an attempt to take care of their editing clients' needs.

POV. See point-of-view shot.

preproduction. The preparatory phase of a show during which the script and money are finalized, talent (actors) and crew hired, locations and schedules locked, and sets, wardrobe, props, etc. created. Preproduction follows the development phase and precedes the production phase.

production. The phase of a show during which the filming takes place on set or location. Also referred to as the "shooting" phase, "the shoot," or "principal photography." Production follows the preproduction phase and precedes the postproduction phase.

raking shot. A tight form of a two-shot, usually (or other shot), that is filmed from the side and favors one character.

reaction. A cut to a participant reacting to something that is happening.

reverse. A cut to the opposite (reverse) angle. The cut can be from the *front* of a character to *behind* the character (or vice versa) or *from* a character (or characters) *to* the character (or characters) they're facing.

seamless editing. See invisible editing.

screen direction. The direction where a character or object enters or exits a shot.

short cut. A cut that has a brief duration — less than two seconds. shot. The footage filmed from camera start to camera stop.

slo mo. Effect where the pace of the action is decreased from what occurred in reality in front of the camera. This retardation is accomplished during editing or, more traditionally, during filming by overcranking — running the film through the camera at a faster rate than it will be played back. Opposite of speed up.

smash cut. Variation on a short cut. An unexpected, lightning-quick cut designed to deliberately jar the audience by zapping the action from one place/object/person/image to another.

special effects house. Facility where effects are created and finalized.

speed up. Effect where the pace of the action is increased from what occurred in reality in front of the camera. This acceleration is accomplished during editing or, more traditionally, during filming by undercranking — running the film through the camera at a slower rate than it will be played back. Opposite of slo mo.

split screen. Dividing the screen into two or more parts with different shots in each division.

still frame. See freeze frame.

subliminal cut. A cut consisting of a few frames which zip by so fast that the viewer is only subliminally (subconsciously) aware of them.

superimposition. Effect where two shots (or more) are held on top of each other full screen.

take. A shot that starts (or ends) with a camera slate (clapstick).

tilt. Shot where camera moves vertically up and down or down and up.

tracking shot, a.k.a. dolly shot. Shot where camera follows the action (often a character) while mounted on a dolly that is pushed along a set of temporary tracks laid down on the ground.

transition effect. Effect, such as a dissolve or wipe, which moves the action from one cut to another.

white out. Effect where a shot cuts or dissolves to white. Often involves organic elements such as a light, a camera flashbulb, or steam.

wide shot (WS). A shot framed wide that encompasses much if not all of the action.

wipe. A transitional effect where the incoming shot replaces the outgoing shot by appearing to wipe (erase) it from the screen.

FILMOGRAPHY: FILM AND EDITOR(S)

* ***Babel*** – Douglas Crise, Stephen Mirrone

Brokeback Mountain – Geraldine Peroni, Dylan Tichenor

Cars – Ken Schretzmann

Corpse Bride – Jonathan Lucas, Chris Lebenzon

‡ ***Crash – Hughes Winborne

Fahrenheit 911 – Kurt Engfehr, Christopher Seward, T. Woody Richman

* ***Finding Neverland*** – Matt Chesse

Harry Potter and the Goblet of Fire – Mick Audsley

** ***Hero*** – Zhai Ru, Angie Lam

Hot Fuzz – Chris Dickens

* ***Into the Wild*** – Jay Cassidy

Kill Bill Vol. 2 – Sally Menke

Knocked Up – Brent White, Craig Alpert

La Vie en Rose – Richard Marizy

Lust, Caution – Tim Squyres

Mamma Mia – Lesley Walker

‡‡ ***Man on Wire*** – Jinx Godfrey

* ***Munich*** – Michael Kahn

*‡ ***No Country for Old Men*** – Roderick Haynes

Paprika – Takeshi Sayama

Pan's Labyrinth – Bernat Vilaplana

Pirates of the Caribbean, Dead Man's Chest – Craig Wood, Stephen Rivkin

Ratatouille – Darren Holmes

Rope – William H. Ziegler

‡ ***Slumdog Millionaire – Chris Dickens

Spider-Man 2 – Bob Murawski

*** ***The Aviator*** – Thelma Schoonmaker

*** ***The Bourne Ultimatum*** – Christopher Rouse

* ***The Constant Gardener*** – Claire Simpson

The Da Vinci Code – Dan Hanley, Mike Hill

* ***The Diving Bell and the Butterfly*** – Juliette Welfling

* ***There Will Be Blood*** – Dylan Tichenor

Underworld Evolution – Nicholas de Toth

* ***United 93*** – Clare Douglas, Richard Pearson, Christopher Rouse

War of the Worlds – Michael Kahn

* Nominated for Academy Award for Best Editing
** Nominated for Academy Award for Best Foreign Language Film
*** Won Academy Award for Best Editing
‡ Won Academy Award for Best Picture
‡‡ Won Academy Award for Best Documentary

BIBLIOGRAPHY

Abeel, Erica. indieWIRE Interview with *The Diving Bell and the Butterfly* Director Julian Schnabel, November 29, 2007.

Apple, Wendy (director). *The Cutting Edge: The Magic of Cinema Editing*. Documentary on DVD available from Amazon, 2004.

Bradford, Steven. "The Blue/Green Screen Page",
www.seanet.com/~bradford/blue_green_screen_visual_effects_1.html

Browne, Steven E. Film – *Video Concepts*. Boston: Focal Press, 1992.

Chandler, Daniel. "The 'Grammar' of Television and Film," 1994,
www.aber.ac.uk/media/Documents/short/gramtv.html
"Devilish Perceptions," *Fear* Magazine, Issue 24 (December 1990).

Chandler, Gael. *Cut by Cut: Editing Your Film or Video*.
Studio City, CA: Michael Wiese Productions, 2004.

Dancyger, Ken. *The Technique of Film and Video Editing. History, Theory, and Practice*. 3rd ed. Boston: Focal Press, 2002.

Dmytryk, Edward. *On Film Editing. An Introduction to the Art of Film Construction*. Boston: Focal Press, 1984.

Goldman, Mia. "Interview with Dede Allen Part 1," *The Motion Picture Editors Guild* Magazine, Vol. 21, No. 4 (July/August 2000).
http://en.wikipedia.org/wiki/Subliminal_message

Lindgren, Ernest. *The Art of the Film*. New York: Macmillan, 1963.

LoBrutto, Vincent. *Selected Takes. Film Editors on Editing*. Westport, CT: Greenwood Publishing Group, 1991.

Masterpiece Theatre website. Production Notes, The Forsyte Saga, Series 1. Fall 2002. *www.pbs.org/wgbh/masterpiece/forsyte/index.html*

McGrath, Declan. *Editing and Post-Production*, Screencraft.
Boston: Focal Press, 1998.

Michele's Blog, "Subliminal Persuasion: Getting the Story a Little Less Wrong," *http://serendip.brynmawr.edu/exchange/node/438*

Millar, Gavin and Karel Reisz. *Technique of Film Editing*. 2nd ed.
Boston: Focal Press, 1995.

Murch, Walter. *In the Blink of an Eye, A Perspective on Film Editing*. 2nd ed.
Los Angeles: Silman-James Press, 2001.

Oldham, Gabriella. *First Cut. Conversations with Film Editors*.
Berkeley, CA: University of California Press, 1992.

O'Steen, Bobbie. *Cut to the Chase*.
Studio City, CA: Michael Wiese Productions, 2002.

Pepperman, Richard D. *The Eye is Quicker: Film Editing: Making a Good Film Better.* Studio City, CA: Michael Wiese Productions, 2004.

Rosenblum, Ralph and Robert Karen. *When the Shooting Stops… the Cutting Begins. A Film Editor's Story*.
New York: Da Capo Press, 1989 (1979).

Tarkovsky, Andrei. *Sculpting in Time*.
Austin, TX: University of Texas Press. 1989.

Thompson, Roy. *Grammar of the Edit*. Boston: Focal Press, 1993.

Truffaut, François. *Hitchcock*. New York: Simon and Schuster, 1966.

Van Sijll, Jennifer. *Cinematic Storytelling The 100 Most Powerful Film Conventions Every Filmmaker Must Know*.
Studio City, CA: Michael Wiese Productions, 2005.

Vokey, J. R. and S. W. Allen. *Psychological Sketches*. 6th ed.
Lethbridge, Alberta: Psyence Ink, 2002.

INDEX

ABOUT THE AUTHOR

It all started in a small drive-in theatre in Santa Rosa, California to paraphrase Ted Baxter from the *Mary Tyler Moore Show.* The author got a job as a cashier at Starvue Motor Movies but was more interested in the projection booth. There she learned base and emulsion, cement and tape splicing, and other 35mm basics. Eventually her union brothers and the town's theatre managers were persuaded to let her in the booth and the union. This meant she got to run *Rocky*, *Star Wars*, and *Saturday Night Fever* for months and take location assignments doing grip, electrical, and craft service work. Much film through projector and two BAs later, she headed for Hollywood and began slipping through studio gates.

Her first job was as an assistant at a sound studio where she transferred 500 tiger growls from ¼" to 35mm on her first day. It was a good place to meet editors and led to her first assistant editor job on the television show *That's Incredible.* From there it was a whirlwind of jobs and trips to the unemployment office.

Gael Chandler has edited comedies, dramas, documentaries, features, corporate videos, and promos and cut on every type of medium: film, tape, and digital. Nominated twice for a Cable ACE award for editing a comedy series, she is a member of the Editors Peer Group of the Television Academy of Arts and Sciences and annually judges the Emmy and College TV awards.

She has taught editing at Loyola Marymount University and California State Universities at Los Angeles, Long Beach, and Northridge and trained hundreds of professionals, professors, independent filmmakers, and students to operate digital editing equipment.

The author has written a handful of feature screenplays, one of which won the Scriptwriters Networks' Producers Outreach Program contest and may yet be coming to a theatre near you. The writing has made her a better editor and vice versa. Her first book, *Cut by Cut: Editing Your Film or Video,* published in 2004, details the editing process from dailies to tube, screen, DVD, or Web. Additionally, she has created numerous online courses on a variety of subjects, including editing.

Chandler has walked the halls of Hollywood, both dark and cluttered with film reels and bright and glittering with Emmys, Clios, and Oscars, and feels dedicated to passing on her knowledge to all who seek to enter the cutting room or understand editing. She continues to live and thrive in Los Angeles. You can contact her via her website at *www.joyoffilmediting.com* or at *info@gaelchandler.com*.

CUT BY CUT
EDITING YOUR FILM OR VIDEO

GAEL CHANDLER

At last: the most complete and definitive book on both the techniques and principles of film and video editing. This "bible" is a highly focused text for beginners and experienced editors alike. No matter what gear you use, Gael Chandler cuts through the clutter and tells you what you need to know to make your work brilliant.

Learn how the skilled editor turns raw footage into a polished show. Discover how to edit action, montage, and dialogue and what's unique to editing drama, documentary, comedy, news, commercials, music videos, and other genres.

With 50 information-packed tables and forms, over 100 original illustrations and photos, and an up-to-date glossary and resource guide, this book is indispensable.

"Whether you're a seasoned professional or just getting started, Gael Chandler's book will serve as a comprehensive guide through the post-production process. This book is a must read for anyone facing the challenge of editing their own film or video project."

– Jay Scherberth, A.C.E.
Friends, Scrubs, Real World, Columbo

"Finally we have a comprehensive text on the subject for every student of editing, written in an understandable manner without sacrificing content. It is what God and DeMille intended."

– Jack Tucker, A.C.E.
Editor and Teacher, CSULB, CSUN, and UCLA

"In one volume, we not only learn how editing is accomplished, but also see how editors apply theory when making cuts. It is a book that will prove invaluable to students just starting out as well as professionals who feel they need a refresher course in this ever-changing industry."

– Dan Watanabe, VP of Development
CRC Entertainment;
Instructor, Los Angeles
Valley College

GAEL CHANDLER has been nominated twice for a Cable Emmy for comedy editing; has edited every type of genre on every medium – film, tape, and digital; and has trained hundreds of professionals and students to put their best cut forward.

FILM & VIDEO BOOKS

TO RECEIVE A FREE MWP NEWSLETTER, CLICK ON WWW.MWP.COM TO REGISTER

SCREENWRITING | WRITING

And the Best Screenplay Goes to... | Dr. Linda Seger | $26.95
Archetypes for Writers | Jennifer Van Bergen | $22.95
Cinematic Storytelling | Jennifer Van Sijll | $24.95
Could It Be a Movie? | Christina Hamlett | $26.95
Creating Characters | Marisa D'Vari | $26.95
Crime Writer's Reference Guide, The | Martin Roth | $20.95
Deep Cinema | Mary Trainor-Brigham | $19.95
Elephant Bucks | Sheldon Bull | $24.95
Fast, Cheap & Written That Way | John Gaspard | $26.95
Hollywood Standard, The | Christopher Riley | $18.95
I Could've Written a Better Movie than That! | Derek Rydall | $26.95
Inner Drives | Pamela Jaye Smith | $26.95
Joe Leydon's Guide to Essential Movies You Must See | Joe Leydon | $24.95
Moral Premise, The | Stanley D. Williams, Ph.D. | $24.95
Myth and the Movies | Stuart Voytilla | $26.95
Power of the Dark Side, The | Pamela Jaye Smith | $22.95
Psychology for Screenwriters | William Indick, Ph.D. | $26.95
Rewrite | Paul Chitlik | $16.95
Romancing the A-List | Christopher Keane | $18.95
Save the Cat! | Blake Snyder | $19.95
Save the Cat! Goes to the Movies | Blake Snyder | $24.95
Screenwriting 101 | Neill D. Hicks | $16.95
Screenwriting for Teens | Christina Hamlett | $18.95
Script-Selling Game, The | Kathie Fong Yoneda | $16.95
Stealing Fire From the Gods, 2nd Edition | James Bonnet | $26.95
Way of Story, The | Catherine Ann Jones | $22.95
What Are You Laughing At? | Brad Schreiber | $19.95
Writer's Journey, - 3rd Edition, The | Christopher Vogler | $26.95
Writer's Partner, The | Martin Roth | $24.95
Writing the Action Adventure Film | Neill D. Hicks | $14.95
Writing the Comedy Film | Stuart Voytilla & Scott Petri | $14.95
Writing the Killer Treatment | Michael Halperin | $14.95
Writing the Second Act | Michael Halperin | $19.95
Writing the Thriller Film | Neill D. Hicks | $14.95
Writing the TV Drama Series - 2nd Edition | Pamela Douglas | $26.95
Your Screenplay Sucks! | William M. Akers | $19.95

FILMMAKING

Film School | Richard D. Pepperman | $24.95
Power of Film, The | Howard Suber | $27.95

PITCHING

Perfect Pitch - 2nd Edition, The | Ken Rotcop | $19.95
Selling Your Story in 60 Seconds | Michael Hauge | $12.95

SHORTS

Filmmaking for Teens | Troy Lanier & Clay Nichols | $18.95
Ultimate Filmmaker's Guide to Short Films, The | Kim Adelman | $16.95

BUDGET | PRODUCTION MANAGEMENT

Film & Video Budgets, 4th Updated Edition | Deke Simon & Michael Wiese | $26.95
Film Production Management 101 | Deborah S. Patz | $39.95

DIRECTING | VISUALIZATION

Animation Unleashed | Ellen Besen | $26.95
Citizen Kane Crash Course in Cinematography | David Worth | $19.95
Directing Actors | Judith Weston | $26.95
Directing Feature Films | Mark Travis | $26.95
Fast, Cheap & Under Control | John Gaspard | $26.95
Film Directing: Cinematic Motion, 2nd Edition | Steven D. Katz | $27.95
Film Directing: Shot by Shot | Steven D. Katz | $27.95
Film Director's Intuition, The | Judith Weston | $26.95
First Time Director | Gil Bettman | $27.95
From Word to Image | Marcie Begleiter | $26.95
I'll Be in My Trailer! | John Badham & Craig Modderno | $26.95
Master Shots | Christopher Kenworthy | $24.95
Setting Up Your Scenes | Richard D. Pepperman | $24.95
Setting Up Your Shots, 2nd Edition | Jeremy Vineyard | $22.95
Working Director, The | Charles Wilkinson | $22.95

DIGITAL | DOCUMENTARY | SPECIAL

Digital Filmmaking 101, 2nd Edition | Dale Newton & John Gaspard | $26.95
Digital Moviemaking 3.0 | Scott Billups | $24.95
Digital Video Secrets | Tony Levelle | $26.95
Greenscreen Made Easy | Jeremy Hanke & Michele Yamazaki | $19.95
Producing with Passion | Dorothy Fadiman & Tony Levelle | $22.95
Special Effects | Michael Slone | $31.95

EDITING

Cut by Cut | Gael Chandler | $35.95
Cut to the Chase | Bobbie O'Steen | $24.95
Eye is Quicker, The | Richard D. Pepperman | $27.95
Invisible Cut, The | Bobbie O'Steen | $28.95

SOUND | DVD | CAREER

Complete DVD Book, The | Chris Gore & Paul J. Salamoff | $26.95
Costume Design 101 | Richard La Motte | $19.95
Hitting Your Mark - 2nd Edition | Steve Carlson | $22.95
Sound Design | David Sonnenschein | $19.95
Sound Effects Bible, The | Ric Viers | $26.95
Storyboarding 101 | James Fraioli | $19.95
There's No Business Like Soul Business | Derek Rydall | $22.95

FINANCE | MARKETING | FUNDING

Art of Film Funding, The | Carole Lee Dean | $26.95
Complete Independent Movie Marketing Handbook, The | Mark Steven Bosko | $39.95
Independent Film and Videomakers Guide - 2nd Edition, The | Michael Wiese | $29.95
Independent Film Distribution | Phil Hall | $26.95
Shaking the Money Tree, 2nd Edition | Morrie Warshawski | $26.95

OUR FILMS

Dolphin Adventures: DVD | Michael Wiese and Hardy Jones | $24.95
On the Edge of a Dream | Michael Wiese | $16.95
Sacred Sites of the Dalai Lamas- DVD, The | Documentary by Michael Wiese | $24.95
Hardware Wars: DVD | Written and Directed by Ernie Fosselius | $14.95

To Order go to www.mwp.com or Call 1-800-833-5738